50 BOOKS FOR LIFE

A Concise Guide to Catholic Literature

50 BOOKS FOR LIFE

A Concise Guide to
Catholic Literature

✦ ✦ ✦

Roy Peachey

First published
by Second Spring, 2019
www.secondspring.co.uk
an imprint of Angelico Press
© Roy Peachey 2019

For information, address:
Angelico Press
169 Monitor St.
Brooklyn, NY 11222
info@angelicopress.com
www.angelicopress.com

978-1-62138-468-7 (pbk)
978-1-62138-469-4 (cloth)
978-1-62138-470-0 (ebook)

Cover design: Michael Schrauzer

CONTENTS

Introduction

Writing at the turn of the nineteenth century, Joseph Joubert argued that the trouble with new books is that they prevent us from reading the old ones. If that was true 200 years ago, the problem is even more acute today. So many books are published each year that, in our struggle to keep up, we often neglect what the past has to offer. That is why, in this short guide, I have tried to provide an accessible introduction to the great tradition of Catholic literature, looking at neglected classics as well as recent bestsellers. Starting in the twenty-first century, I want to take you on a journey backwards in time in search of some of the greatest books ever written. Condensing the whole history of Catholic literature into 50 books has not been an easy task. But being forced to select, I have had to go back to basics and ask some fundamental questions. What gives a book staying power? What is it about a story that makes it worth reading? What can literature give us?

In one of his short story collections, George Mackay Brown lamented the fact that much "of the old story-telling has withered before the basilisk stare of newsprint, radio, television." However, by traveling back through history, we can rediscover at least some of what we have lost. Of course, a short book like this cannot be comprehensive—it is an introduction and nothing more—and I am acutely conscious of the gaps and omissions. But to anyone who is upset by the absence of, say, Greene, Bernanos, or Mauriac, I have to point out that great works from earlier times, including Langland's *Piers Plowman*, Chaucer's *Troilus and*

Criseyde, and St Thomas More's *Utopia*, also failed to make the cut. That doesn't mean they are not worth reading. Far from it. It simply means that we have to start somewhere, and the danger is, as Joseph Joubert warned us, that we are often quite happy to start with what is readily available, which means that we never get round to reading old books. That is why this guide starts with contemporary literature—with the books most of us are likely to pick up first—and then takes us back in time to Classics we may admire but never read and also to Classics that we may have forgotten altogether. By turning history on its head, I hope to shake out some unexpected treasures from its trouser pockets.

I have kept this guide short because it is only a guide—it is meant to point beyond itself—yet maybe it is not the shortness of the guide that requires explanation, but the very notion of Catholic literature, which is a term in search of a definition. Though widely pursued, it remains an elusive quarry, showing different faces to different people as it runs before them. So what do I mean by it?

First, I believe that Catholic literature must be seen as a tradition. No book is an island, entire of itself, to misquote John Donne. Books don't emerge out of a void. They are all, to some degree or other, responses to previous books. There is a wonderful moment at the very end of Chateaubriand's *Atala* when the narrator meets some displaced Natchez Indians. They have lost virtually everything, but, even so, they have managed to hang onto the bones of their ancestors, which they carry with them wrapped in animal skins. Reflecting on their example, the narrator realizes: "I am less fortunate in my exile, for I do not carry with me the bones of my fathers." So it is with Catholic literature: unless it carries the bones of its ancestors with it, it ceases to exist in any meaningful sense.

Catholic literature differs from many of its secular counterparts in positively welcoming the books that have come before. There is no anxiety of influence here. To read the work of Gerard Manley Hopkins, to give just one example, is to be drawn into the work of St Robert Southwell, Old English poetry, early Welsh literature, and, of course, the Bible. In fact, the Bible is the foundational text for all the authors represented here. Sometimes obviously, sometimes obliquely, they all draw on the riches of the Sacred Scriptures.

But there is more to Catholic literature than a series of responses to earlier writing: Catholic literature also draws on, responds to, and is sometimes even an analogue of the liturgy. David Jones saw the liturgy itself as "a supreme art-form," an art-form that cannot simply be read or spoken but that demands to be lived (or "enacted"). In one way or another all Catholic literature stands in some relation to it. Imagine Catholic literature as a chasuble, the outer vestment worn by priests when they celebrate Mass. Chasubles can be found in museums, removed from their original context. They are still beautiful in their display cabinets, but, separated from the liturgy for which they were created, they no longer have any real sense of significance. We could say the same of literature. Cut off from the life of the Church, books can still be beautiful, powerful and affecting, but it is only when they are brought back into the life of the Church that they can gain any lasting significance.

Catholic literature is like a beautiful chasuble, but we have to acknowledge that it is a garment that has been frayed, damaged, and even torn in two (though we can still hope that it will be restored to wholeness one day). That is why there is a case for including works by Orthodox writers like Eugene Vodolazkin and Fyodor Dostoevsky in any list of

Catholic literature. In fact, we could go further and include literature from the Coptic world, from the Ethiopian Church, and even from certain strands of Protestantism. I have limited myself to books from the Catholic world in this guide purely for reasons of space.

Our literary chasuble has been torn and it has frayed. Nonetheless, the threads that have come away from the original garment retain a certain beauty that can only be enhanced when they are re-incorporated into the original vestment. That is why I have included books like Cormac McCarthy's *The Road* in this guide. McCarthy may not be an orthodox Catholic, but there is a strong case to be made for reading *The Road* in the light of the history of Catholic literature. In the bright light of the Faith the darkness of *The Road* is softened, if not banished entirely. Out of the bleakness of McCarthy's post-apocalyptic vision, hope is still able to emerge.

The more we read in the Catholic literary tradition, the more we see a continuity of purpose and expression. And the more we read in the tradition, the deeper our understanding and appreciation of each individual book becomes. So make use of this guide as you will. Read it from cover to cover or dip into it in spare moments. And when you have finished, read the books themselves. You will not be disappointed. The literature to which this little guide points is great enough to last a lifetime.

Kyung-Sook Shin
Please Look After Mom (2008)

Like the Church itself, Catholic literature knows no boundaries. That is why I am starting in South Korea, with Kyung-Sook Shin's *Please Look After Mom*, which won the Man Asian Literary Prize in 2011 and has sold over two million copies worldwide. From its very first lines, *Please Look After Mom* takes us into unfamiliar territory: "It's been one week since Mother went missing," we are told. "The family is gathered at your eldest brother Hyong-chol's house, bouncing ideas off each other. You decide to make flyers and hand them out where Mother was last seen."

For those of us who aren't South Korean women or whose mothers haven't gone missing, this is extremely disconcerting, but there is no escape, for the second-person narrative draws us straight into the middle of the crisis. We are not only with the characters as they struggle to make sense of what has happened to their mother, but we are now a member of the family with a responsibility to find the missing woman. And all we know is that, in her confused state, she wandered off from Seoul's train station when no one arrived on time to collect her. Simultaneously inside the fiction and detached from it, we are as powerless as the rest of the family while the search continues.

As the plot unfolds, we inevitably find ourselves thinking about our own relationships. Have we neglected our own mothers? Are we blind to the needs of older generations? The novel draws us in only to push us back out again. These questions are insistent, partly because the structure of the narrative forces us to keep questioning. Having gotten used to the second person narrative, we find that the next section of the novel is written in the third person from the perspective of one of the sons. Then the viewpoint changes again: in the following section we are back in the second person, though this time we are placed in the husband's shoes. When eventually we hear Mom's own voice, we get to know her as though for the first time. The mystery of the person is deeper than we had ever imagined.

There is great anguish in the book, but the author does not leave us bereft, for in the last section of the book we leave Korea for Italy. To be more precise, she takes us to the Vatican and Michelangelo's great Pietà in St Peter's Basilica. As we are shown Jesus's broken body in the arms of his mother, we see suffering in another light and are reminded that the Holy Family can help us make sense of our own earthly relationships. With the suffering of the Korean family placed in the context of another relationship, the loving bond between Our Lord and Our Lady, the novel ends not with anguish but with love and hope. *Please Look After Mom* is a wonderful novel in many ways, but perhaps its greatest value lies in that simple reminder: that salvation ultimately comes through love, not through books.

Cormac McCarthy
The Road (2006)

The Road starts with the end. The end of the world. Or, at least, the end of the world as imagined by Cormac McCarthy. After some unspecified catastrophe, an unnamed father and son trek across a barren landscape in what the father fears is likely to be a fruitless search for salvation. Most people are dead; the land is dead; and anything remotely resembling civilization is dead too.

The man and his son have only themselves and a few basic goods that they drag along in a deeply symbolic supermarket trolley. The trolley and what is possibly the world's last can of Coca Cola are all that remain of the consumerist world of capitalist America.

But something greater than consumer goods has survived the disaster. The love of a father and son lies at the heart of this terribly bleak novel. What survives in the post-apocalyptic landscape is a love that is clarified by the horror: "If he is not the word of God," the father says of his boy, "God never spoke." This may not be theologically sound, but the man's heartfelt cry takes us out of the secular world of the modern novel into a place that is clearly "Christ-haunted," to use Flannery O'Connor's fine phrase.

McCarthy does not deal in certainties, but the world he describes, a world in which "the frailty of everything [is] revealed at last," where cannibalism is rife and children are roasted on spits, is also shot through with what he calls in *The Sunset Limited* "the lingering scent of divinity." The father rails against the God in whom he no longer believes, but God is revealed through words—McCarthy's stark, stunning prose—and, most importantly, through actions. This is why the end of the novel is so important and yet so often misunderstood.

The novel ends with hope, with a redemptive adoption, with a woman bringing the boy back from the horrific abyss which is the only life he knows. The novel ends, it could be argued, with a re-imagining of Hemingway's "Big Two-Hearted River" where "things were older than man and they hummed of mystery."

Georg Lukács once argued that the novel as a genre is "the epic of a world that has been abandoned by God," but God has not been entirely driven out of the novelistic world. Despite the horror, despite the bleakness, despite the nihilism, something greater than these survives in McCarthy's fiction. Love is the deep mystery that hums at the heart of this great novel.

The Road doesn't end with the end of the world. Love doesn't end with the end of the world. The end really does turn out to be a beginning.

Les Murray
New Collected Poems (2002)

Are some types of literature more inherently Catholic than others? It seems a strange question to ask, but Australian poet Les Murray had an answer. "Prose is protestant-agnostic/," he wrote, "story, explanation, significance,/but poetry is Catholic;/poetry is presence."

"Presence" was a key concept for Murray precisely because he believed that there is a limit to what poetry can achieve. For Murray, as for many other Catholic writers, literature can take us only to the edge of mystery, since presence resides "in the unsayable, in all that lies beyond even the achieved poem's reach," as literary critic Steven Matthews puts it. This is not to downplay the importance of writing, because presence can only be reached through material objects like words. What really matters may be (currently) beyond our reach, but poetry can take us towards it. Literature can be sacramental.

Murray's poetry helps us to understand what literature can and cannot do. He believed that when we use words to explain, we limit ourselves and our writing. To describe the "greyer, flatter speech of functional prose and rational dominance," Murray used the term "Narrowspeak." However, when we place ourselves before the mystery of creation—when we accept our limits—our poetry can breathe beauty, goodness and truth. Murray called this language "Wholespeak."

Writing in a way that was sometimes reminiscent of Gerard Manley Hopkins, Murray traced a path from the natural to the supernatural, from poetry to presence. For Murray, poetry and true religion were inextricable. His books were dedicated "to the glory of God," and he even went so far as to claim that "any real religion is a big slow poem, while a poem is a small fast religion." Taking the idea further in a poem called "Poetry and Religion," he wrote that "Religions are poems. They concert/our daylight and dreaming mind, our/emotions, instinct, breath and native gesture/into the only whole thinking: poetry."

The afterlife was another preoccupation in his verse, and the topic often brought out Murray's wry sense of humor: "Just two hours after/Eternal Life pills came out/someone took thirty," he wrote in one devastatingly short meditation. In another poem he argued that although "The secular withholds any obeisance/that is aimed upwards..., we require an afterlife/greater and stranger than science gives us now,/life like, then unlike/what mortal life has been." The afterlife may be a difficult concept for the secular culture Murray critiqued, but poetry can make it easier to comprehend: "A poem is an afterlife on earth," he claimed.

Many Catholics have written great poetry in the 21st century but Murray was perhaps the most distinguished of them all, having won the T. S. Eliot Prize, been awarded the Queen's Gold Medal for Poetry, and been tipped for the Nobel Prize. That his name is not more widely known has more to do with the low regard in which poetry is generally held than with the undoubted quality of his work. His presence, like the presence of which he writes, deserves to be much more widely known.

George Mackay Brown
Beside the Ocean of Time (1994)

George Mackay Brown was a poet but, unlike Les Murray, he was a novelist too. He wrote many fine books but only gained the recognition he deserved when his last book, *Beside the Ocean of Time*, was shortlisted for the Booker Prize in 1994. The novel centers around Thorfinn Ragnarsson, an Orkney islander who prefers dreaming to school. Or, to put it another way, he is a boy who, despite his teacher's best efforts, refuses to give up on his "quest for the grail of poetry," as the narrator puts it toward the end of the novel. Like Mackay Brown himself, Thorfinn is not restricted by the time and place in which he is rooted. As he dreams, he finds himself in one historical adventure after another, traveling to Byzantium with a Viking band and to Bannockburn with an ineffective Orcadian knight, to name but two.

Beside the Ocean of Time is an elegy for lost time and for a place that has lost touch with time. But it is more than just an elegy, because it takes seriously what is beyond time. Becoming increasingly aware that "the life of man ... is a brief voyage, with an ocean of eternity, the many-voiced sea, all around," Thorfinn becomes wise beyond his years and, we might say, beyond his time.

Beside the Ocean of Time often has an elegiac feel, but there is hope too. Having been liberated from Stalag 29B at the end of World War II—a powerfully unexpected twist to the novel—Thorfinn ekes out a living by writing historical thrillers, though what he really wants to do is "to dredge something rich and strange out of the mythical past of the islands" that have now been denuded of people because of the need for an air force base. Realizing that "there is a great mystery in this connection between music and death and time and the food that the earth yields for the nourishment of men," he comes to believe that the task "will almost certainly be too difficult for him"; he wonders, "even if it does come off, what will his publisher say about whimsy like this?"

In the end, Thorfinn does manage to write "a novel that yearned towards poetry." As he predicted, it is not a popular success but it does preserve something of the fragile beauty of the Orkneys. The miracle is that, in *Beside the Ocean of Time*, George Mackay Brown also made "something of what was left" of the islands but he won literary plaudits while doing so. Writing from the margins of literary society, he knew that what is marginal can also become central. Rooted in time and place, he reached out beyond both, sensing that "the hard rock of language, mined and labored at, might break open and reveal the ore; and out of that gold every poet fashions the chalice sufficient for his offering."

But, as a Catholic author, he also knew that the "grail itself is never to be found this side of time." Catholic literature always points beyond itself, and there are few better examples of how it does so in the twentieth century than in the work of this wonderful Orcadian author.

Muriel Spark
The Prime of Miss Jean Brodie (1961)

"What was your biggest influence?," a visitor asks Sister Helena, one of the central characters in Muriel Spark's novel. "Was it political, personal? Was it Calvinism?"

"Oh no," the nun replies. "But there was a Miss Jean Brodie in her prime."

Miss Jean Brodie is one of the great characters in twentieth-century fiction, and the girls in the novel who come under her influence at an impressionable age never forget her. She is a great character but she is also a complex and dangerous woman. We learn very early in the novel, for example, that she is an admirer of Mussolini and that she is molding her own pupils into a group of *fascisti*. However, her fascistic tendencies don't tell the whole story. Believing that beauty, truth and goodness should be the end at which true education aims, she takes her students out of the mundane world of Calvinist Edinburgh but, having a warped understanding of beauty, truth and goodness, she can only take them so far. She is a wonderfully charismatic teacher, but she cannot lead her students to the truth because she has lost her own way.

How to make sense of this spinster schoolmistress who shaped her pupils for life only to be betrayed by one of "the Brodie set," as the girls were known, is the question that dominates the book. The narrative structure encourages us to search for a pattern that makes sense of the reality that Spark's characters daily experience but only dimly understand. Sandy Stranger, who later becomes Sister Helena, is particularly "fascinated by this method of making patterns with facts" and eventually finds a vocation that enables her to make sense of both patterns and facts. As a nun, she discovers what Jean Brodie never does: that the Church "could have embraced, even while it disciplined, [Jean Brodie's] soaring and diving spirit." The teacher could have been a great saint: as it was she died embittered and alone.

The Prime of Miss Jean Brodie is not so much a novel about Catholicism as a novel that is haunted by Calvinism. For much of the book Sandy yearns not so much for the truth of Catholicism as for a falsehood to oppose: "it was the religion of Calvin of which Sandy felt deprived, or rather a specified recognition of it. She desired this birthright; something definite to reject." Having been born and educated in Edinburgh before later converting to Catholicism, Muriel Spark felt this desire too and in her novels she maintained a continual argument with Scottish Calvinism. When the Junior School teachers say "good morning" in *The Prime of Miss Jean Brodie,* they do so "with predestination in their smiles," and Miss Brodie herself is constantly tempted by a particular delusion of grandeur: she "thinks she is Providence . . . , she thinks she is the God of Calvin, she sees the beginning and the end."

Muriel Spark was fascinated by the interplay of predestination and free will. Her novels are sites on which a battle is constantly being fought between the author's pseudo-Calvinist control of her characters, her quasi-divine foreknowledge of those characters' destinies, and the freedom they retain or achieve having been created. As often as not, these battles are reflected in the structure of the novels too. In *The Prime of Miss Jean Brodie* the reader is pulled back and forward in time, seeing the end and the beginning, the end in the beginning, predestination and free will in a beautifully constructed literary and theological dance.

So the question that the visitor asks Sandy/Sister Helena—the question that also ends the book—is an astute one. Calvinism, and the struggle against it, had a huge influence on both Sandy and her creator. And so too did Miss Jean Brodie in her prime.

Gabriela Mistral
Complete Poems (1958)

The Nobel Prize for Literature is a curious award that has been won by some unexpected authors. Though it may not be an entirely objective marker of quality, it is still worth drawing attention to at least some of the Catholic authors to whom it has been awarded. The Chilean poet Gabriela Mistral won the prize in 1945, with the Swedish Academy, which referred to her as the "spiritual queen of Latin America," noting her "remarkable pilgrimage from the chair of a schoolmistress to the throne of poetry."

But Mistral went on another pilgrimage too. Born in rural Chile into a devoutly Catholic family, she was particularly influenced by her grandmother who read to her from the Bible and encouraged her to learn and recite passages by heart. In one of her poems, Mistral wrote about this early devotion:

> Bible, my noble Bible, magnificent panorama,
> where my eyes lingered for a long time,
> you have in the Psalms the most burning of lavas
> and in its river of fire I lit my heart!
>
> You sustained my people with your strong wine
> and you made them stand strong among men,
> and just saying your name gives me strength;
> because I have come from you I have broken Destiny.
>
> After you, only the scream of the great Florentine
> went through my bones.

Though she was also influenced by Dante, "the great Florentine," Mistral wandered away from Catholicism for a while as she developed a career as a devoted teacher and published her first poems and prose pieces. However, she later returned to the Faith, becoming a lay Franciscan. Like many other Catholic authors (including Julien Green and François Cheng, for example), she was strongly influenced by St Francis and wrote about him. In returning to the Faith, she also turned a poetic corner. At the end of her first collection of poetry, *Desolación*, she announced her intentions:

> I hope God will forgive me for this bitter book. I leave it behind me, as you leave the darkened valley, and I climb by more benign slopes to the spiritual plateaus where a wide light will fall over my days. From there I will sing the words of hope, I will sing as a merciful one wanted to do, for the consolation of men.

Though she never stopped writing about the desolation of the poor and neglected—especially women and children—Mistral certainly added a newly hopeful Franciscan strain to her poetry. She also continued her religious and poetic pilgrimage while traveling across the world: she lived at various times in Mexico, the USA, Italy, Puerto Rico, Spain, and Brazil, serving as the Chilean consul in various cities as well as the Chilean representative to the United Nations in her later years. However, the pull of her early childhood in rural Chile never left her. It was a place she returned to in her poetry and it is there that she was buried after her death in the USA in 1957.

J. R. R. Tolkien
The Lord of the Rings (1954–55)

Writing to his son Michael in the dark days of World War II, J. R. R. Tolkien offered the greatest encouragement he could find: "Out of the darkness of my life, so much frustrated, I put before you the one great thing to love on earth: the Blessed Sacrament.... There you will find romance, glory, honour, fidelity, and the true way of all your loves upon earth, and more than that: Death: by the divine paradox, that which ends life, and demands the surrender of all, and yet by the taste (or foretaste) of which alone can what you seek in your earthly relationships (love, faithfulness, joy) be maintained, or take on that complexion of reality, of eternal endurance, which every man's heart desires." This statement is worthy of slow, considered contemplation. It is a reminder, if a reminder is needed, of how deeply Catholic an author Tolkien was.

But Tolkien was writing more than just letters to his children at this time. He was also working on *The Lord of the Rings*, a book in which religion is conspicuous by its absence, not because it was unimportant to him but because it was so deeply embedded in his life that it shaped every aspect of his work without needing to appear explicitly. We can see this by looking at the structure of the book. As Tom Shippey reminds us, *The Lord of the Rings* is not a novel in any straightforward sense: "the basic structural mode of *The Lord of the Rings* [is] the ancient and pre-novelistic device of entrelacement." According to Shippey, it was Tolkien's use of this "chronological leapfrogging" that enabled him to create a book in which the necessarily limited perspectives of the characters pointed, albeit obliquely, to a larger reality that could only be understood from a perspective outside the fiction itself.

Over and above the actions of the book, as understood by the characters within it, there is a larger pattern, a shape, a meaning that is revealed through the decisions the characters make and the actions they perform. What is hidden from them is glimpsed by us and, by literary extension, by God himself.

When Frodo tells Gandalf, "It's a pity Bilbo didn't kill [Gollum] when he had the chance," he receives this reply: "Pity? It was pity that stayed Bilbo's hand. Many that live deserve death. Some that die deserve life. Can you give it to them, Frodo? Do not be too eager to deal out death in judgment. Even the very wise cannot see all ends. My heart tells me that Gollum has some part to play yet, for good or ill before this is over. The pity of Bilbo may rule the fate of many." And, of course, that turns out to be true, though not even Gandalf is able to see that far at the start of the book.

According to Valentine Cunningham, Professor of English Language and Literature at Oxford University, novels "have rights to that designation only insofar as they display their origins in and their debt to the Northern European Protestant matrix." For Tolkien, that was a good enough reason not to write a novel. To create *The Lord of the Rings*, he turned instead to an earlier, neglected Catholic tradition of storytelling. In so doing, he reshaped the literature of the twentieth century and created a modern masterpiece.

Flannery O'Connor
A Good Man is Hard to Find (1953)

In "Some Aspects of the Grotesque in Southern Fiction," Flannery O'Connor wrote, "All novelists are fundamentally seekers and describers of the real, but the realism of each novelist will depend on his view of the ultimate reaches of reality." What many readers value in her work is the absolute clarity of the reality—the sharp, precisely observed details of the American South—and that wider reach into the fundamental realities that so much modern fiction does its best to ignore. One of O'Connor's favorite quotations was from St Gregory of Nyssa: "every time the sacred text describes a fact, it reveals a mystery." The job of the author, as she saw it, was not to pin down the mystery but to open it up, avoiding the temptation "to enshrine the mystery without the fact." Through the earthiness of her writing we reach the spiritual.

Like Tolkien, O'Connor was acutely aware of the limitations of the secular age in which, and for which, she was writing, though her literary response to these limitations was quite different. In one of her finest stories, "A Good Man is Hard to Find," for example, she writes about a very ordinary family in a very ordinary part of the country that is caught up in extraordinary events. Her own deadpan summary of the story in *Mystery and Manners* is that it is about "a family of six which, on its way driving to Florida, gets wiped out by an escaped convict who calls himself the Misfit." It is a violent story but also—which you might not realize from O'Connor's own description—extremely funny.

O'Connor was an early product of the Iowa Writer's

Workshop. Her short stories in particular are therefore extremely well crafted. In "A Good Man is Hard to Find" the sentences are beautifully constructed, the comic timing is immaculate, and the plotting is exquisite. What she does better than almost any other twentieth-century author is to nail a character with a phrase. Take this skewering of the Grandmother's restricted view of the world, for instance. Speaking to her son about her grandchildren, she says: "You all ought to take them somewhere else for a change so they would see different parts of the world and be broad. They never have been to east Tennessee."

"A Good Man is Hard to Find" abounds in darkly comic moments, from the Grandmother's choice of "a big black valise that looked like the head of a hippopotamus" to the moment the cat she has smuggled into the car escapes and leaps onto her son's shoulders, causing him to crash. However, "A Good Man is Hard to Find" is not simply a tragicomedy. The violence in the story is there to return "my characters to reality and [to prepare] them to accept their moment of grace. Their heads are so hard that almost nothing else will do the work." Before she is killed, the Grandmother realizes her responsibility for what has happened and, more surprisingly, her kinship with the Misfit. The conventions of modernist realism are transcended for a moment and the furthest, or most intimate, reaches of reality open up for her. The story is no longer what we thought it was. In reading it, we, like the Grandmother, have been changed.

David Jones
The Anathemata (1952)

Arguably the greatest Catholic author of the twentieth century, David Jones is still comparatively unknown. Though he first made his reputation as an artist, working with, and learning from, Eric Gill at Ditchling, he was a maker in the broadest sense of the word rather than just an artist, an engraver, or a poet. In fact, one of Jones's strengths is that he is so difficult to pin down. He was a great artist, which is why his work can now be seen at Tate Britain among other galleries, but his art is not always easy to categorize. He was also a great poet, but his finest work challenges the very distinction between poetry and prose. He was a war poet who published his first great work, *In Parenthesis*, almost twenty years after World War I, and a modernist who continued to write dense, complex books when literary trends had moved on.

Jones's work certainly emerges out of the modernist mainstream but, unlike most other modernists, he saw and understood the world theologically. This is particularly clear in *The Anathemata*. The fundamental question for the poet (who above all is a "sign-maker"), Jones argues in his preface, is how "to lift up valid signs" in an age when signs are no longer valid. He believed that there had been a "Break," a time "in the nineteenth century, [when] Western Man moved across a rubicon which, if as unseen as the 38th Parallel, seems to have been as definitive as the Styx." Living on the wrong side of that Break meant that his task as a sign-maker was significantly more difficult than it had ever been for writers before.

He found his answer to the question of how to lift up valid signs, and indeed to every question, in the liturgy and especially in the Mass, which is why *The Anathemata* begins and ends with the priest, as *alter Christus*, lifting up an "efficacious sign." *The Anathemata* is shaped by the Mass and is a profound meditation on it. The action, such as it is, takes place between the consecration of the bread and the wine, and the complex explorations that form the basis of the poem can best be understood as a working-out of what it means for people in one place and at one time to be drawn into what is beyond time. Or, to put it more accurately, it is about being drawn into relationship with Him who is beyond time and yet has drawn time into Himself by entering into it.

That is why the book begins with the priest reciting the Prayer of Consecration: "We already and first of all discern him making this thing other. His groping syntax, if we attend, already shapes: ADSCRIPTAM, RATAM, RATIO-NABILEM..." That is why it continues with a description of the Mass: "In the prepared high-room/he implements inside time and late in time under forms indelibly marked by locale and incidence, deliberations made out of time." That is why it ends with priest's/Christ's action: "He does what is done in many places/what he does other/he does after the mode/of what has always been done."

The Anathemata is a book that demands to be read in a way we have largely forgotten in our hectic age. The denseness of the poetry slows us down. The breadth of the argument compels us to read expansively, while the frequent notes draw us away from the broad sweep of the text and back into the world. In a phenomenally complex way, Jones creates a commentary on the Mass that is also an analogue of it. And if that seems a complicated way of putting it, *The*

Anathemata is a complex book that demands complex readings! There is nothing else like it in modern literature.

Evelyn Waugh
Brideshead Revisited (1945)

According to Evelyn Waugh, the theme of *Brideshead Revisited* is "the operation of divine grace on a group of diverse but closely connected characters." Such a theme is not a typical feature of twentieth-century fiction, so what did Waugh mean by this statement? How exactly does divine grace work upon his characters?

The most obvious example of grace at work in the characters' lives comes at the end of the novel when the dying Lord Marchmain makes the sign of the cross, in response to the priest's request for a sign that he is sorry for his sins: "Well, now, and that was a beautiful thing to me. I've known it happen that way again and again," the priest says.

Lord Marchmain is certainly not the only character to respond to the prompting of divine grace. As the family waits by Marchmain's deathbed, Charles Ryder also gets down on his knees and prays, "longing for a sign" and asking God, "if there is a God, [to] forgive him his sins, if there is such a thing as sin." Unlike Lord Marchmain, Charles is an outsider. He scarcely fits in at Brideshead or at Oxford and he cannot make head nor tail out of Catholicism when he first stumbles across it. Nonetheless, the divine angler slowly reels him in, needing no more than a twitch upon the thread to be able to bring him back from the ends of the earth. The metaphor is G.K. Chesterton's, as appropriated by Waugh. Just as Charles is gradually drawn into a great tradition of which he is hardly aware, so too did Waugh conceive of *Brideshead Revisited* within a tradition of great Catholic literature.

Two other great presences haunt Waugh's novel: John Henry Newman and the liturgy itself. When, at the start of Book Three, Charles's wife tells him that he hasn't changed at all he agrees, but when he quotes Newman—"It's the only evidence of life"—we realize that change is happening, whatever both of them think. Waugh never comments directly on the operation of divine grace, but if we are attentive we can catch the hints.

Cordelia, Sebastian Flyte's ardent younger sister, has already been trying to convert Charles, encouraging him to go to Tenebrae because "if you had you'd know what the Jews felt about their temple. *Quomodo sedet sola civitas* ... it's a beautiful chant. You ought to go once, just to hear it." There seems little chance of that happening but, chastened by life, Charles is slowly reeled in by the divine angler. Later in the book, after "nearly ten dead years," he reflects on what has happened to him: "'Here I am,' I thought, 'back from the jungle, back from the ruins. Here where wealth is no longer gorgeous and power has no dignity. *Quomodo sedet sola civitas*' (for I had heard that great lament, which Cordelia once quoted to me in the drawing-room of March-main House, sung by a half-caste choir in Guatemala, nearly a year ago)."

What matters, in other words, is what lies beyond the novel: great Catholic writers; the great liturgical tradition; and, most importantly, the liturgy itself, which continues throughout history, solid if not unchangeable. Writing late in his life about the liturgical changes that followed the Second Vatican Council, Waugh said that "Of the extraneous attractions of the Church which most drew me was the spectacle of the priest and his server at low Mass, stumping up to the altar without a glance to discover how many or how few he had in his congregation; a craftsman and his apprentice; a man with a job which he alone was qualified to do." This was not the complaint of a bitter old man. The liturgy had always mattered to him. It had always been there, no matter how many or how few there were in the congregation. It was what had shaped his great novels, *Sword of Honour* and *Brideshead Revisited* especially.

Which brings us back to the theme of this great novel. *Brideshead Revisited* really is a book about the operation of divine grace on a group of diverse but closely connected characters. The grace of God continues to work behind the words of the novel. In literature as in life, we have to look carefully if we are to see it, but whether we see it or not, it is always there.

Takashi Nagai
The Bells of Nagasaki (1949)

On August 9th, 1945, while "crowds of Christians, wearing white veils, prayed and made reparation for the sins of the world" in Urakami Cathedral, an atomic bomb was dropped on Nagasaki. A few hundred meters from the epicenter of the explosion, Dr Takashi Nagai, a nuclear physicist and dean of the radiology department, was choosing X-rays to use in his teaching at the University of Nagasaki. Though he was wounded in the blast, he immediately began to mobilize the few survivors to treat the injured and put out the fires that were threatening to engulf the building and burn those trapped inside. *The Bells of Nagasaki* is his book about the hours, days, and months that followed.

How do you respond to the incomprehensible? How do you write about the unspeakable? Nagai's answer was to write as a scientist and to respond as a Catholic. One of the most remarkable aspects of this remarkable book is Nagai's scientific objectivity in the face of the horror. In fact, he wrote that the dropping of the bomb "was a precious experience for us." Why? Because "placed on the experimentation table, we could watch the whole process in a most intimate way." On page after page, he explains with an almost total absence of emotion the physical effects of the bomb, ranging from a cut to his head—"An artery in my temple had been cut. But since it was a small artery, I thought my body would hold out for about three hours. Sometimes I felt my own pulse and then went on treating patients"—to the devastating impact of radiation sickness.

But *The Bells of Nagasaki* is far from being a cold, scientific treatise. Rather it is a deeply Catholic book, an account of love in action: "Like a mosquito whose legs have been plucked off, like a crab whose claws have been torn away, we faced a multitude of wounded people, helpless and empty-handed. It was really primitive medicine that we were now reduced to. Our knowledge, our love, our hands—we had only these with which to save the people." Stripped of all inessentials, life was reduced to the absolute fundamentals, enabling Nagai to discover for the first time his true vocation as a doctor, a Catholic, and, ultimately, a prophetic writer.

When the war ended, Nagai returned to the center of Nagasaki, building himself and his surviving children a small hut in which to live. He had already contracted leukemia, probably as a result of his radiological work, so he dedicated his last years to caring for his children and writing many powerful books. Nagai was no ordinary author. He also quickly became a symbol of the new Japan, a living example of forgiveness, love and understanding.

Nagai died in 1951. He was and continues to be an inspiration to many. Sadly only a few of his books have been translated into English. We are fortunate that *The Bells of Nagasaki* is one of them.

Ernest Hemingway
A Farewell to Arms (1929)

Ernest Hemingway is not often thought of as a Catholic novelist, but the impact of his Catholic beliefs can be seen throughout *A Farewell to Arms*: in the sympathetic portrayal of a priest; in a description of the narrator's near-death experience on the Italian front line; but especially in the journey the narrator, Frederic Henry, goes on during the course of the novel.

Let us look at two parallel episodes: the first (in some ways the most shocking episode in the book) is when Henry shoots one of his comrades in the back as he runs away and then shows no remorse for his action. The second appears later in the novel when Henry himself is shot at by his own side, apparently for abandoning his company.

What we make of these parallel episodes is very much left up to us. Since Hemingway didn't like to "write like God," as he once said, we are forced back onto our own resources. The starkness of the style, the absence of all extraneous details, and the refusal of the detached first-person narrator to pass judgment force us to plunge into the morally murky world he describes before we can come to conclusions ourselves.

Nonetheless, despite the absence of direction from the narrator, we are likely to conclude that to do to others as you would have them do to you is an inescapable law of life. It seems that Frederic Henry comes to think the same, for though the bare narrative continues throughout the novel, the narrator does not remain entirely detached. In fact, his journey (or pilgrimage) leads us and him toward a Catholic ending.

As an ambulance man at the front line, Henry is unable to respond emotionally to the deaths of many of his comrades-in-arms and his senses become dulled, but as he is nursed back to health he finds himself being slowly overtaken by love. Emotional detachment is therefore no longer possible, especially when, at the end of the novel, he is confronted by the possibility that his wife might die.

The passages that describe his inner turmoil as he waits in a Swiss hospital are among the finest in this wonderful novel. But bleak as they are, they do not plunge us into an abyss of hopelessness, for Henry himself has changed, not wholly but enough to suggest that he is on his way home, that Chesterton's great angler is reeling him in too.

Getting the end of the novel just right meant a great deal to Hemingway. In fact, he rewrote the ending 47 times! The version that made it into the published work is heart-breakingly bleak. Henry's wife's death is narrated with terrible restraint and the novel ends with the narrator apparently unable to cope, walking back to his hotel in the rain. There is no sign of the hope of the resurrection: what we get instead is a very human response that suggests the breaking-down of the emotional detachment that had all but destroyed Henry during the war. There is love and there is pain. Whether there is also hope is left up to us, the readers, to decide.

Sigrid Undset
Kristin Lavransdatter (1922)

"It was in winter that the islanders gathered round the hearth fire to listen to the stories," George Mackay Brown wrote in the forward to his *Winter Tales*. "Harvest was gathered in. The ears that had listened only to necessary farming and fishing words all the year of toil and ripening were ready for more ancient images and rhythms."

Brown was writing about the Orkneys but his words could be applied equally well to the Scandinavian world about which Sigrid Undset wrote so beguilingly. In fact, we could go further: if ever there was a book whose ancient images and rhythms deserved to be read or heard over the long, dark months of winter it is Undset's *Kristin Lavransdatter*.

Perhaps better than any other work in modern fiction, *Kristin Lavransdatter* creates a wholly authentic Catholic world, a world in which the liturgical calendar permeates every aspect of life, in which priests and religious are not objects of suspicion but simply part and parcel of lived experience. Writing about fourteenth-century Norway, Undset captured the era beautifully. She escaped the twin dangers of pastiche and historical nostalgia by writing with great precision about food, weather and customs, and by creating utterly convincing characters.

Kristin herself is a character we get to know and love over time. As we journey with her through the novel, we learn about her strengths and desires, and about her foibles and failures too. She is a strong, determined, and multifaceted woman who changes deeply as the novel unfolds. When we first meet her she is passionate and somewhat naïve, but through experience—sometimes bitter and sometimes joyful—she develops both knowledge of the world and true wisdom.

What is perhaps most remarkable about *Kristin Lavransdatter* is that Undset created a wholly convincing Catholic world without ever coming close to hagiography. She created an admirable heroine who has as many faults as we do, a protagonist whose story we want to follow over the 1,124 pages of this three-part novel—which is why I shall resist the temptation to simplify her life, or Undset's novel, by giving an inadequate summary here.

George Mackay Brown concluded the forward to his *Winter Tales* by claiming that "Every community on earth is being deprived of an ancient necessary nourishment. We cannot live fully without the treasury our ancestors have left to us." What he wrote is true, though he could have added that for those who have ears to hear and eyes to see the ancient necessary nourishment can still be found. And Sigrid Undset's great novel—an epic tale written in an age when epics were no longer in fashion—is as good a place as any to begin.

Paul Claudel
The Tidings Brought to Mary (1912)

The Tidings Brought to Mary is not a play about the Annunciation, as the title might suggest, but a drama set in France during the fifteenth century. The early years of that century were difficult ones: Joan of Arc had not yet appeared to restore King Charles VII to his rightful position on the throne, and the Western Schism was still unresolved. Without a king in Paris or a pope in Rome, French Catholics struggled to find a sure compass.

Though this historical setting has an impact on the events of the play, Claudel's focus is elsewhere. He begins with an encounter between Violaine, a young woman who is about to be married, and Pierre de Craon who, we quickly discover, once attempted to rape her. Violaine, who becomes an increasingly saintly character as the play progresses, not only forgives him but even gives him a kiss out of pity when he reveals that he has contracted leprosy. In kissing him, however, she also contracts the disease.

What this opening suggests is that the play will be an intensely physical drama. What is perhaps less obvious is Claudel's desire to explore how the physical and the supernatural meet, *The Tidings Brought to Mary* being, in his own words, "the representation of all the human passions in their relation to the Catholic plan."

We see more of these human passions when Violaine's sister, Mara, enters the play. Seeing the kiss, Mara manages to separate Violaine from her fiancé, Jacques Hury, so that she can take Violaine's place. Violaine's life then enters a downward spiral: forced away from the family home and from all human company by her leprosy, she becomes a cave-dwelling hermit while Mara marries Jacques.

All this might seem long way from the tidings brought to Mary, but what makes the play truly remarkable is the way it is shaped by the liturgy and, in particular, by the Angelus that resounds throughout the play, drawing characters and audience out of the world of the theater into the life of the Church. Or, to put it another way, just as we and the characters are drawn into the spiritual through the physical, so too are we drawn into the supernatural through this naturalistic, though highly poetic, drama.

The central moment of the play takes place on Christmas Eve when Mara, carrying her dead baby, visits the leprous Violaine, whom she has not seen for seven years. Believing that the baby's death has been caused by her mistreatment of Violaine, she begs her sister to bring the child back to life. As Joan of Arc takes Charles VII to be crowned at Rheims, Mara reads the Christmas office to Violaine, who is now blind, and as we listen to readings from Isaiah, the Gospel of St Luke, St Gregory the Great, and St Leo the Great, we hear the angels sing and see the baby restored to life, though now with Violaine's blue eyes rather than Mara's black eyes. It is a remarkable scene that lifts the play out of its fifteenth-century setting into the eternal.

G.K. Chesterton
Charles Dickens (1906)

It might seem strange in a survey of Catholic literature to choose one of Chesterton's non-fiction works rather than his *Father Brown* stories or a poem like "The Ballad of the White Horse." There are two reasons why I have done so. The first is to make the point that our conception of literature has become progressively narrower over the years, to our great loss. Our forebears quite happily understood sermons, essays, and letters to be literary forms, to say nothing of sagas, romances, and epics. A second reason for choosing Chesterton's study of Charles Dickens is given by the literary scholar and priest Fr Ian Ker, who argues convincingly that "the author of the Father Brown stories and even of *The Man Who Was Thursday* (1907), his best novel, is indeed a fairly slight figure," but that Chesterton the non-fiction writer "can be mentioned without exaggeration in the same breath as Carlyle, Ruskin, Arnold, and especially, of course, Newman."

So what do we find in Chesterton's critical study of Charles Dickens? I am tempted to reach for a Chestertonian paradox and say that we don't learn a great deal about Dickens but do learn a huge amount about Chesterton, yet that wouldn't be entirely true. Rather we learn a huge amount about both Dickens and Chesterton, and about literature and religion and a great deal more besides. With an ability to get to the nub of Dickens' work without being dazzled by his brilliance, Chesterton saw what made Dickens great and what could have made him greater.

In his chapter on *The Pickwick Papers*, for example, he

wrote not just about Dickens' breakthrough book but also about the nature of the novel and of popular religion. In fact, being Chesterton, he linked the two with his trademark linguistic skill: "Both popular religion, with its endless joys, and the old comic story, with its endless jokes, have in our time faded together. We are too weak to desire that undying vigour.... The grand old defiers of God were not afraid of an eternity of torment. We have come to be afraid of an eternity of joy."

Or, to take another example, Chesterton undermines Dickens' unthinking English Protestant assumptions by demonstrating that, in his defense of Christmas, he was in fact the inheritor of a great European Catholic tradition: "He could only see all that was bad in mediaevalism. But he fought for all that was good in it. And he was all the more really in sympathy with the old strength and simplicity because he only knew that it was good and did not know that it was old. He cared as little for mediaevalism as the mediaevals did."

Chesterton is clearly one of the great Catholic writers of the early twentieth century, even though he didn't convert to Catholicism until 1922, after he had written many of his most famous works. Like Sigrid Undset and John Henry Newman, two great literary converts, he can be said to have written himself into a change of religion. Where his imaginatively-charged intellect led him, he eventually followed. What he gave us in his generous study of Dickens was the first part of that journey, clear evidence that non-Catholic as well as Catholic authors can lead the open-minded to the glories of the Church.

Henryk Sienkiewicz
Quo Vadis? (1896)

The fourth of our trilogy of Nobel Prize-winning authors (after Ernest Hemingway, who won in 1954, Gabriela Mistral, who won in 1945, and Sigrid Undset, who won in 1928) is Henryk Sienkiewicz, who won the prize in 1905. His greatest novel, *Quo Vadis?*, begins with a short explanation:

> Tradition has it that, as Saint Peter was fleeing from Rome to escape the persecutions of the Emperor Nero, he met Christ on the Appian way, and asked Him, "Quo vadis?" ("Whither goest thou?"); to which the Saviour replied, "To Rome, to be crucified anew, inasmuch as thou art abandoning my sheep." Hence the title of the following work.

However, anyone picking up this book to read about the life and death of St Peter is in for a surprise, for the first part of the book at least. Neither St Peter nor St Paul is mentioned in the first 100 pages, and even when we do meet St Peter for the first time, we see him from a distance and his words are given to us secondhand, in reported speech.

What we get instead is a stunning introduction to Nero's Rome, full of vivid characters and historical details, that sets the scene for the persecutions that arrive later in the novel. The novel begins with Petronius, who is chiefly remembered as the author of the *Satyricon*, and one of his protégés, Vinicius, who has fallen in love with (or maybe is lusting after) a barbarian known as Lygia. Except we soon discover that Vinicius is the real barbarian (in his attempts to abduct the young woman) and Lygia (who comes from the country of the Lygians, which is modern-day Poland) is the truly civilized one. Her manners, her bearing, and especially her Christian faith set her apart from the sordid barbarism of Nero's Rome.

What follows is a remarkable story that is both extremely exciting and utterly convincing. We are drawn into the decadence of the era so that when eventually we see St Peter we get a vivid sense of the countercultural newness of Christianity in the Roman world. Traveling with Vinicius to the catacombs for the long-expected visit of St Peter to Rome, we enter an underground world that operates by different rules from the decadent mainstream, where power lies with Rome's underclass and where political intrigue is absent.

However, we also begin to see that Nero's Rome and Christian Rome do not, and cannot, exist in parallel. As he leaves the catacombs, Vinicius is shocked to see two Roman soldiers kneel down for a blessing from St Peter; as the underground movement gains strength, it begins to have a visible impact on the Roman superstate. Conflict is, therefore, inevitable, and when it comes it is terrible. I won't give any more plot spoilers here because *Quo Vadis?* is a genuine page-turner that will keep you on the edge of your seat, even when you know where the plot is ultimately heading. Some Nobel Prize winners have sunk into total obscurity: here is one whose great reputation is thoroughly deserved.

Gerard Manley Hopkins
The Wreck of the Deutschland (1876)

In late 1875 a short report appeared in the press about the shipwreck of the *Deutschland*, a steamer that had been en route from Germany to the USA, in a terrible storm off the English coast, and the loss of many lives "by exposure or drowning." It was, it seemed, a tragic accident that would soon be forgotten. However, the shipwreck and the deaths were destined not to be forgotten, for news of the tragedy deeply affected a young Jesuit priest who also happened to be one of the greatest poets of the nineteenth century: Gerard Manley Hopkins.

Among the victims of the shipwreck were five Franciscan nuns who had been exiled from Germany as a result of Bismarck's *Kulturkampf*. For Hopkins, the nuns were not victims of a senseless tragedy but modern-day martyrs whose example could inspire Catholics in his own country, since they too were struggling to establish themselves in the face of a hostile establishment.

However, rather than produce a piece of religious propaganda, Hopkins created an incredibly powerful—and, in some ways, remarkably dense—poem that addressed issues of life and death, of conversion and martyrdom, and of time and eternity. Hopkins' poetic technique and linguistic inventiveness were so far in advance of his times (because they were rooted in pre-Reformation Welsh and English poetry) that it wasn't until the twentieth century that they began to be appreciated and imitated by writers as diverse as Dylan Thomas and George Mackay Brown. In fact, "The Wreck of the Deutschland" was not published in his own lifetime.

What Hopkins attempted to show in the poem is how salvation comes through suffering, how a human tragedy can actually be a divine triumph. The poetic journey begins with a disaster—Bismarck's anti-Catholic laws—and appears to finish with another—the terrible storm that wrecks the ship—but Hopkins's account differs dramatically from the newspaper reports of the time. The passengers "fought with God's cold—/And they could not and fell to the deck/ (Crushed them) or water (and drowned them) or rolled/ With the sea-romp over the wreck"; but that is not the end of the story, for one of the nuns ("a lioness") rose up and called on God's name, reminding the poet and the people of England in whose waters she was drowned that a "feast followed the night," and that the ship, rightly understood, could become "an ark/For the listener." That is why Hopkins was able to end his poem, just as he began it, with a prayer. Praying to the martyred nun, he wrote: "Dame, at our door/Drówned, and among óur shoals,/Remember us in the roads, the heaven-haven of the reward." It was a fine way to end one of the greatest poems of the nineteenth century.

John Henry Newman
Callista: A Tale of the Third Century
(1864)

Brought up as an Anglican, Gerard Manley Hopkins was received into the Church by perhaps the greatest of the Anglican converts: John Henry Newman. Newman is best known for his great theological works and for his luminous *Apologia Pro Vita Sua*, a book setting out the story of his conversion from Anglicanism to Catholicism that is widely regarded as one of the classics of the nineteenth century. This was an astounding feat given the fact that it was written under incredible time-pressure: responding to a scurrilous review by Charles Kingsley, Newman brought out seven pamphlets in seven weeks, often working for twenty hours a day to ensure he met his deadlines. Even so, as Frank Cottrell Boyce has written, "despite the frenzy and sweat in which it was written—the book itself is calm. Serene in fact. And spacious and generous."

It wasn't just the speed at which he wrote that made Newman such a remarkable writer: he was one of the greatest prose stylists of the century and one of the most versatile writers too. In addition to his theological and autobiographical works, he also wrote wonderful hymns, poetry, and two novels: *Loss and Gain*, a fictional portrayal of an Anglican convert to Catholicism; and *Callista: A Tale of the Third Century*. Newman was not alone in using every tool at his disposal to evangelize the culture of his time. Nicholas Wiseman, the first Cardinal Archbishop of Westminster, also wrote a novel, *Fabiola*, about the early Christian martyrs.

Callista is not the novel Newman's enemies might have expected. The book begins by focusing on Agellius, a wealthy North African Christian who falls in love with Callista, a sophisticated pagan woman. While his Christian faith pulls him in one direction his erotic desires pull him in another. This is no hagiography, in other words. The Christians in Newman's novel are as likely to conform to the comfortable, pagan society in which they live as they are to resist it courageously.

However, there are times when resistance is called for. When the Emperor Decius demands that everyone in the empire make public sacrifices to the gods or face torture and execution, a pagan mob takes matters into its own hands and sets on the Christians. As Callista tries to warn Agellius, the crowd seize her instead. In prison she starts to have doubts about her pagan commitment and refuses to offer a public sacrifice as proof that she has not been tainted by Christianity, even though it might result in her being condemned to death.

While in captivity she reluctantly reads a copy of St Luke's Gospel that has been smuggled into prison and finds an account "of a new state and community of beings, which only seemed too beautiful to be possible," and an ideal "to which her intellect tended, though that intellect could not frame it." Here was a consummation of everything that paganism at its best had offered and, more importantly, an introduction to "One who was simply distinct and removed from anything that she had, in her most imaginative moments, ever depicted to her mind as ideal perfection." With incredible bravery and single-mindedness, she follows the truth as she discovers it in the pages of the Gospel even though she knows it will result in her death. What began as a book about Christian complacency becomes a bold call to arms. *Callista* is a novel of the third century but one of the nineteenth century as well. Though hardly read now, it speaks powerfully to our times too.

Alessandro Manzoni
The Betrothed (1827)

When Alessandro Manzoni died, his funeral in Milan was attended by thousands of people because his greatest book, *The Betrothed*, had made him an Italian hero—so much so, in fact, that Verdi composed his famous Requiem in 1874 to commemorate the anniversary of his death, commenting that *The Betrothed* "is not just a book, it offers consolation to the whole of humanity." Written during the Risorgimento, *The Betrothed* spoke powerfully to its age, but it has equally successfully outlived the time in which it was written and is now widely regarded as one of the classics of world literature.

The novel is set in seventeenth-century Lombardy, and the love story at its heart takes place against a setting of political chaos in Italy, the Thirty Years' War, and an outbreak of the plague. However, what is most striking about the book on first reading is not the historical background but the wonderfully drawn characters and the engaging narrative voice. *The Betrothed* is often a wonderfully funny book. It is also a long novel, but so sure is the author's touch that we willingly follow where he leads. This is a book that is a real pleasure to read.

It is also a deeply Catholic novel. The Capuchin monk Fr Cristoforo is a wonderful creation, simultaneously human and holy. He is the perfect foil for Don Abbondio, the cowardly parish priest whose weakness sets the story in motion. But there is more to the novel's Catholicism than its monks, nuns, and priests. Manzoni's deep faith (which was all the stronger from having been rejected in his youth) permeates the whole book. What the narrator says about the Christian religion can be equally well applied to the novel itself:

> She is like a great road, which a man may find after wandering in the most tangled labyrinth, amid the most dangerous precipices, and once he has taken one stride along it, he can walk on safely and gladly, and be sure of a happy end to his journey.

The journey Manzoni described did end happily, though his protagonists undoubtedly suffered terribly on the way. Nonetheless, suffering can lead to wisdom, which is why they are able to offer us great advice in the last pages of the book:

> But after a long debate, and much heart-searching they came to the conclusion that troubles very often come because we have asked for them; but the most prudent and innocent of conduct is not necessarily enough to keep them away; also that when they come, through our fault or otherwise, trust in God goes far to take away their sting, and makes them a useful preparation for a better life.

François-René de Chateaubriand
Atala (1801)

In his youth, Chateaubriand wandered far from the Church, embracing a skepticism typical of the age. However, the deaths of his mother and sister provoked a spiritual crisis and conversion; in his own words, "I wept and I believed." Reacting strongly against the cold rationalism of the so-called Enlightenment, he came to see Christianity as a religion that was, first and foremost, beautiful, which is why he turned so readily to fiction.

Chateaubriand's rich Romanticism may not be to everyone's taste, but there is a great deal more to *Atala*, his most influential book, than Romantic aestheticism. Having spent five months in America exploring the Northwest Passage, Chateaubriand returned to France with a deep fund of experiences on which to draw when eventually his life and his faith came into harmony. Everything came together in *Atala*, a novella in which he aimed to demonstrate "the harmonies of the Christian religion with the scenes of nature and the passions of the human heart."

Atala begins with "a Frenchman named René [who], driven by his passions and sorrows, arrived in Louisiana. He traveled up the Mississippi as far as the land of the Natchez, and asked to be considered as a warrior by this nation." Chactas, an old Indian man who was once a prisoner of the French, then told him the story of his life and, especially, of his love for Atala, the Christian daughter of a rival tribe. Rescuing Chactas shortly before her people were due to have him killed, Atala fled with him into the wilderness but was tormented by the fact that she loved a man she could never marry, since he was not a Christian like her.

In the wilderness they met an old hermit, Fr Aubry, who brought them to his cave. In many ways this missionary priest is the real hero of the novel. Not only did he live for others, but he also modeled the life that Chactas and Atala needed in their precarious situation: the type of life that Chateaubriand thought was needed after the horrors of the French Revolution. Fr Aubry had not fled the disorder of the human passions but redeemed them: "You could see that his days had been hard, and the wrinkles on his brow were evidence enough of the deep scars of passion healed by virtuous living and by the love of God and man."

In the priest's grotto, the story takes a dramatic twist that I will not reveal here, other than to say that in his response to this dramatic moment in the plot and to further revelations about the past, Fr Aubry remained constant, confronting "the dangers of excess and the want of light in matters of religion" with the wisdom that comes from age, suffering and service. As I wrote in the introduction, the novel ends with an almost Tolkienian moment of sorrow. In the winning of one great battle, much had been lost. But through the example of the faithful Natchez Indians who carry the bones of their ancestors with them, even when everything else is lost, Chateaubriand gives us an image of hopeful continuity that is as relevant today as it was in the dark days that followed the French Revolution.

Sor Juana Inés de la Cruz
The Divine Narcissus (1690)

Sor Juana Inés de la Cruz was a remarkable writer in seventeenth-century Mexico. Her talent was spotted at an early age and she was brought to the viceregal court, where she wrote poetry and theatrical works. She then became a nun and scholar. Her cell was luxurious, containing works of art, mathematical and musical instruments, and some 4,000 books. She continued to write in the convent until, in her early forties, she sold her library, gave the proceeds to the poor, and tended to plague victims instead, before contracting the disease herself and dying a heroic death.

A lot of nonsense has been written about Sor Juana but, as recent scholarship has shown, she was clearly a devout and orthodox nun whose *autos sacramentales*, or Eucharistic dramas written for the festival of Corpus Christi, deserve to be much better known. One of the most remarkable of these was *The Divine Narcissus*, which takes Ovid's story of Narcissus's self-love and transforms it into an account of the love of Christ for his people as seen most especially in his death and resurrection and as represented in the sacrifice of the Mass—Ovid's pagan metamorphosis becoming the transformation of bread and wine into the body and blood of Christ.

In her Eucharistic drama, Sor Juana uses the beauty of Narcissus as a way of presenting the beauty of Christ; what Narcissus sees reflected in the water is not himself but fallen humanity, which he loves with such a complete love that he cannot be parted from it. Tempted by Echo (a figure of the devil in Sor Juana's retelling), Narcissus achieves his victory through his death and resurrection, paving the way for the appearance of the Host:

> (a float with the fountain appears and next to it, a chalice with a host suspended above it.)

Grace

> See, at the crystal rim
> of the clear, bright fountain
> the beautiful white flower
> of which the lover said:

Narcissus

> This is My Body and My Blood,
> which I sacrificed for you
> through many martyrdoms. Do this
> in remembrance of my death.

The Divine Narcissus is a striking reworking of the Ovidian myth that constantly surprises its audience. The force of Sor Juana's intelligence and her dramatic and poetic skill shine through this work, which must have had a powerful catechetical effect if it was indeed ever performed. It would be a mistake, though, to emphasize the originality of the work. This was not Sor Juana's aim: she was much more interested in drawing on an established literary tradition that reached from Ovid to Pedro Calderón de la Barca via St Thomas Aquinas, for it is with his great *Pange lingua* that her play ends, placing *The Divine Narcissus* squarely in the great tradition of Catholic literature that always draws from, and returns to, the work of the Church.

Wu Li
Singing of the Source and Course of Holy Church (late 17th century)

One of the glories of the Catholic Church is that it is catholic or, to put it another way, universal. And the universality of the Church goes back a lot farther than most people realize. There were, for example, Catholics in China as early as the seventh century, though Christianity only really took off in the sixteenth century with the arrival of Matteo Ricci and other Jesuit missionaries. The Jesuits were strikingly successful in China, though they never managed to convert any of the emperors as they had hoped. Nevertheless, as recent historical research has shown, they did make a great impact in the countryside, away from the imperial court, gaining many converts from among both the educated elite and ordinary citizens. One of these converts was a famous artist and poet called Wu Li.

Wu Li was one of the six Orthodox Masters of early Qing Dynasty painting in China. After converting to Christianity, he entered the Society of Jesus in 1682 and was ordained as a priest in 1688. However, even after he became a priest, Wu Li did not stop painting or writing poetry. Quite the opposite. Recent scholars have argued that he was the father of Chinese Christian poetry and that his Christian faith enabled him to reshape early Qing art. His paintings can now be seen in galleries across the world, ranging from the Metropolitan Museum of Art in New York to the Shanghai Museum. His poetry is less well known, but it too is worth tracking down. The most ambitious and successful of his works is "Singing of the Source and Course of Holy Church," a series of twelve

8-line poems, which attempts to distill the essentials of Christianity into the *shi* style of traditional Chinese verse.

Wu Li begins and ends his sequence of poems in Heaven, the place where we should "seek true blessings and true joy," with a description of a palace, enclosed within twelve walls, in which our Holy Mother is surrounded by the saints. This is the source of Holy Church that the title speaks of. The other ten poems, each written in strict *shi* style, describe the course of Holy Church. Moving from the divine plan prepared before the foundation of the world to the creation and the Incarnation, Wu Li then describes his own conversion. After establishing that "the achievements and fame of this ephemeral world are like the footprints of geese on snow," Wu Li moves onto poems that focus on the Holy Trinity and the Eucharist before returning to the goal of every Christian: Heaven itself.

The highly compressed and allusive nature of classical Chinese poetry is a real problem for translators. However, even in English translation, we are able to get a sense of Wu Li's incredible achievement. As a poet, he established a new direction for his countrymen to follow. As an artist, he is still revered as a master. Some of his paintings and poems have been lost, and we know very little about his priestly ministry, but, given the richness of what does survive, we can be extremely grateful for these unexpected gems of Catholic art and literature.

John Dryden
The Hind and the Panther (1687)

The greatest poet and dramatist of his time, John Dryden shocked many people in Restoration England by converting to the Catholic Faith when James II became king. Fending off accusations that he had done so for merely expedient reasons, he tried to show that his conversion was genuine, as it really was. Out of this controversy emerged his longest poem, "The Hind and the Panther," which presents the religious controversies of the age in allegorical form, with the Hind representing the Catholic Church and the Panther the Church of England. The two animals are introduced at the beginning of the poem:

> A Milk white *Hind*, immortal and unchang'd,
> Fed on the lawns, and in the forest rang'd;
> Without unspotted, innocent within,
> She fear'd no danger, for she knew no sin.
> Yet had she oft been chas'd with horns and hounds
> And Scythian shafts; and many winged wounds
> Aim'd at her Heart; was often forc'd to fly,
> And doom'd to death, though fated not to dy.

The Panther, by contrast, is a complex beast: an undoubted danger to the Hind and yet a far nobler animal than the bears, boars and other beasts that Dryden used to describe continental Protestantism:

> The *Panther* sure the noblest, next the *Hind*,
> And fairest creature of the spotted kind:
> Oh, could her in-born stains be washed away,
> She were too good to be a beast of Prey!
> How can I praise, or blame, and not offend,

Or how divide the frailty from the friend?
Her faults and vertues lye so mix'd, that she
Nor wholly stands condemn'd nor wholly free.

"The Hind and the Panther" is a poem in three distinct sections, and Dryden packed a huge amount into his 2,600 lines of verse. I shall therefore have to restrict myself to just a few comments. The first is to point out that the theological content of the poem is quite remarkable. To find a discussion of the Real Presence in verse form is not what we are used to today, and yet Dryden does not shirk from the task, explaining to his Anglican readers the reasonableness of the Catholic position:

Could He his god-head veil with flesh and bloud
And not veil these again to be our food?
His grace in both is equal in extent;
The first affords us life, the second nourishment.
And if he can, why all this frantick pain
To construe what his clearest words contain,
And make a riddle what He made so plain?

The poem also enacts the mysteries it celebrates. Margaret Anne Doody has pointed out that "It tells a story . . . an incomplete story, taking place in a still moment of emblematic history that seems to cover an almost endless amount of imaginative time." She also argues that the Hind doesn't win the debate outright; though it is a response to the religious controversies of the time, Dryden's poem never descends into mere polemic. Instead, "The justification of the Hind is held in suspension, belonging to eternity. The real close cannot be expressed here and now. The poem ends by pointing us elsewhere." That alone marks it out as a thoroughly Catholic work of art and places it firmly in the center of the great tradition of Catholic literature.

Hans Jakob Christoffel von Grimmelshausen
The Adventures of Simplicius Simplicissimus (1669)

There has been a protracted debate about the history of the novel. The tradition with which many of us grew up—that the novel was a post-Protestant, largely Anglophone affair that started with Daniel Defoe, Samuel Richardson, and Henry Fielding—has come under sustained attack in recent years, with many critics writing about the novels of Ancient Greece, Catholic Europe and East Asia. The genre is a lot more diverse and interesting than we have sometimes been led to believe.

Before Defoe, Richardson, or Fielding was writing, Johann von Grimmelshausen was already a household name on account of his picaresque novel, *The Adventures of Simplicius Simplicissimus*. Grimmelshausen was born near the beginning of the Thirty Years' War, which tore Europe apart along religious lines. Dragooned into the fighting at the age of ten, he experienced the full horrors of that terrible war but somehow managed to channel them into an astounding piece of fiction that became an instant success and has remained so ever since.

At some point in his life, Grimmelshausen converted from Protestantism to Catholicism, but his work is a long way from being a piece of Catholic propaganda. In fact, what marks it out is its relentless focus on human weakness and the depravity of human behavior across the religious divide.

The novel begins with a bleak and horrifying account of

an unprovoked attack on the farm where Simplicius's family lived. In a passage that describes a scene depressingly familiar to twenty-first-century readers, Grimmelshausen writes about murder, rape, and torture as simple matters of fact. The young hero of the story, who has already been brutalized by his upbringing, escapes and is given a name for the first time by a hermit he encounters in the woods. The hermit is his first teacher: from him Simplicius learns not only how to read but also how to be. However, when the hermit dies, Simplicius is thrown back on his own devices and begins to live a wild and often dissolute life.

Many of the episodes that follow are wildly implausible. Some are funny. Others are disturbing. We encounter Simplicius as a rogue, usually though not always a lovable one. It is these episodes—the travels, the tall tales, the improbable adventures—that are largely responsible for the book's long-term popular success.

But what makes the book really interesting is the way it ends. Or, rather, the ways it ends. Eventually Simplicius is as sickened by his own life and exploits as his most censorious readers are. Having already converted to Catholicism and then quickly lapsed, he flees the corrupting influence of Europe and ends up on an island in the Indian Ocean. There he lives as the hermit had lived at the start of the book. On the island he writes the story of his life and tells us how we are to read it:

> If someone finds and reads it today or tomorrow, either before or after my death, I ask him not to become irritated if he finds words in it that are not polite to speak, let alone to write. ... A well-meaning Christian reader will probably be astonished and praise divine mercy when he finds that a man as bad as I was could still receive the grace of

God to abandon the world and live in a way which helps him to reach eternal glory and (with the help of the sufferings of the Redeemer) gives him the hope of reaching a blessed Eternity and a holy end.

And so the book ends. Except it doesn't, because Grimmelshausen added a further narrative of a Dutch sea captain who finds Simplicius on his paradisal island. It is this Dutch Protestant narrator who shows us how to interpret the work of the Catholic hermit. Stumbling on Simplicius in the darkness, he needs light from the hermit to escape the cave in which he finds himself. With his men all driven mad, he needs the knowledge only Simplicius can supply to restore them to their right minds. That is why out of the darkness and depravity of the Thirty Years' War a light emerges, dim and wavering but still unquenched. It is only when Simplicius, and we his readers, emerge from the horrors he has described so well that we can begin to find the path to a future free from the bitter ugliness of sin. After the darkness of the events described with such gusto in the book, the light shines brighter at its end.

Richard Crashaw
Poems (mid-17th century)

Born almost 100 years after the start of the Protestant Reformation, Richard Crashaw grew up in a strongly anti-Catholic household. The opinion that prevailed in his home, and in England as a whole at that time, was summed up in a line from a poem he wrote in his 20's: "To be a true Protestant is but to hate the pope."

However, a significant minority in the Church of England, including William Laud, who became Archbishop of Canterbury in 1633, had become disillusioned with mainstream Protestantism and were searching for a way to restore "the beauty of holiness" to the Church without having to burn their bridges entirely by returning to Rome. After becoming a fellow of Peterhouse, Cambridge in 1635, Crashaw quickly emerged as an important figure in this High Church movement, restoring what were widely felt to be Catholic devotional objects to Little St Mary's, the church next door to Peterhouse, when he became curate there.

He didn't get away with his actions for long. With the start of the Civil War raising tensions, Laudian Cambridge became a target. Parliamentary commissioners ransacked Little St Mary's in 1643, tearing down crucifixes and other objects of devotion. Crashaw was forced out of Cambridge and shortly afterwards left the country, emerging in Paris three years later, by which time he had converted to Catholicism. Traveling to Italy, he became canon at the Santa Casa di Loreto, which enshrines the house where Our Lady was said to have been born and received the Annunciation. He died a few months later at the age of 36.

Told like this, his life seems a tragic failure, but during those last difficult years Crashaw wrote and published many wonderful poems which made a big impact on his contemporaries and on future generations, despite the continuing prejudice against English Catholic poets, especially those writing in a so-called baroque style.

Crashaw had a great devotion to Our Lady, and the opening of "In the Glorious Assumption of Our Blessed Lady" is typical of his poetic approach:

> Hark! She is call'd, the parting hour is come;
> Take thy farewell, poor World, Heaven must go home.
> A piece of heavenly earth, purer and brighter
> Than the chaste stars whose choice lamps come to light
> her,
> While through the crystal orbs clearer than they
> She climbs, and makes a far more Milky Way.

As this poem suggests, much of Crashaw's work draws directly on the great traditions of Catholic literature and liturgy. Among his work are poems in honor of St Teresa of Avila and poetic translations of the Stabat Mater, the Dies Irae, St Thomas Aquinas's hymns, and several psalms.

His translation of Psalm 137 is particularly moving; its plaintive song of an exiled people became a favorite of the struggling recusant community. It is not difficult to hear an echo of Crashaw's suffering and that of the English Catholic community in lines such as these:

> They, they that snatch'd us from our country's breast
> Would have a song carved to their ears.

Crashaw must have been tempted to hang up his harp too, but like the Jewish exiles, he turned to song to inspire his co-religionists, to recall better times, and to praise God:

Sing? Play? To whom (ah!) shall we sing or play,
   If not, Jerusalem, to thee?
Ah! Thee Jerusalem! Ah! Sooner may
    This hand forget the mastery
      Of Music's dainty touch, than I
      The music of thy memory.
Which, when I lose, O may at once my tongue
   Lose this same busy-speaking art,
Unperched, her vocal arteries unstrung,
    No more acquainted with my heart,
      On my dry palate's roof to rest
      A withered leaf, an idle guest.

Crashaw was one of the greatest poets of the seventeenth century, but, as this translation shows, he also knew that poetry has its limits. That is why both his life and his work remain as an inspiration to this day.

Pedro Calderón de la Barca
The Prodigious Magician (1637)

The golden age of Spanish classical theater lasted from the late sixteenth century to the mid-seventeenth. Arguably the greatest playwright of this time was Pedro Calderón de la Barca, who wrote for the royal court before being ordained to the priesthood in 1651, from which time he wrote only religious dramas, notably the *autos sacramentales* which he created for the feast of Corpus Christi each year.

However, even before his ordination he wrote religious as well as secular pieces for the theater, including *The Prodigious Magician*, which he wrote for performance in Yepes, near Toledo, as part of its Corpus Christi celebrations in 1637. Rather than focus on the Eucharist, Calderón wrote about Saints Cyprian and Justina, who were said to have been martyred during the reign of the Emperor Diocletian.

In Calderón's retelling, Cyprian begins the play as a pagan philosopher who is searching for the unknown God he finds described in the work of Pliny the Elder. To divert him from his quest, the Devil appears disguised as a fine gentleman and engages him in debate. However, such is the strength of Cyprian's intellect, and such is the strength of his longing, that he defeats his hellish adversary in this verbal duel, leaving the Devil to search for other ways of diverting him from the truth.

Having failed to sway Cyprian's intellect, the Devil decides to attack his senses instead, hoping that if Cyprian falls in love with Justina, a beautiful Christian, his intellect will be overwhelmed by his passion, destroying both Justina and himself.

Since Justina has already been subjected to the unwanted attention of Laelius and Florus, two of his friends, Cyprian offers to intervene on their behalf to resolve their dispute, only to find himself smitten with passion for the pure and beautiful woman. Seeing that the door to Cyprian's soul has been pushed open, the Devil attacks once more, though in a different disguise, offering to teach Cyprian his diabolical arts so that he can ensnare Justina. Cyprian is therefore tempted into selling his soul to the Devil (writing his name in blood on the terrible contract) before joining him in his cave for a year until he is ready to strike his innocent victim.

However, what neither Cyprian nor the Devil had bargained for was Justina's virtue, which is strong enough to repel the former's spells and the latter's temptations. She also becomes the means by which Cyprian is saved. In Christ both his mind and his heart are restored, which allows him to find fulfillment in martyrdom, along with Justina, the shedding of his blood erasing the bloody contract he signed with the Devil.

Calderón's play constantly defies modern expectations. For example, what Calderón focuses on at the end of the play is not the drama of Cyprian and Justina's martyrdom but the identity of the prodigious magician himself. Pulling a rabbit from his theatrical hat, it is only in his very last lines that he reveals the prodigious magician of the title to be neither the pagan Cyprian nor the Devil, but God himself, whose magic is of quite another order, even if it may sometimes be dimly glimpsed in the wonders of the theater.

St Robert Southwell
Poems (late 16ᵗʰ century)

On February 21, 1595, a young missionary priest was hanged at Tyburn in London. His crime was "noe other, but to labour for the salvation of soules, and in peaceable and quiet sort to confirme them in the auntient Catholique Faith," as he wrote in one of his last letters. At the age of 34, Robert Southwell made the ultimate sacrifice.

Southwell was not alone in being martyred for the Faith in Elizabethan England, but he was unique in the manner in which he carried out his mission. During his six years as a fugitive priest in his homeland, he not only said Mass, heard confessions, and brought comfort to his co-religionists: he also wrote for them.

His writings circulated in manuscript form during his lifetime but, remarkably, they were also printed by both Catholic and Protestant presses immediately after his death, though the Protestants tended to drop the more obviously Marian aspects of his work.

Southwell wrote some powerful prose but he is chiefly remembered for his wonderful poetry. His most well-known poem is "The Burning Babe," an audacious Christmas poem that is unlikely to feature in any greeting card. While the poet is shivering in the snow, he feels a sudden heat and, looking up, sees a "pretty babe all burninge bright." The child is in tears, not because of the flames but because while "newly borne in fiery heates I frye/Yet none approach to warme their hartes or feele my fire but I." The babe seems to be suffering in vain and so he tells the poet, in a remarkable development of the image, that "as nowe on fire I am to worke them to their good / So will I melt into a bath to washe them in my bloode." What begins as a comforting Christmas scene ends with a shocking picture that calls to mind the full force of the redemption story.

Southwell was a master of striking imagery. In another poem on the nativity of Christ, for example, he imagined the Christ child in the manger and, reminding his readers of the manger's original purpose, finished his meditation in this way:

> Man altered was by synn from man to best [i.e. beast]
> Bestes foode is haye haye is all mortall fleshe
> Now god is fleshe and lyes in maunger prest
> As haye the brutest sinner to refreshe.
> O happy feilde wherein this foder grewe
> Whose taste doth us from beastes to men renewe.

Again the imagery jolts us out of complacency into a renewed appreciation of the Eucharist.

Southwell is perhaps best known for his imaginative recreations of Biblical scenes, drawing on his training as a Jesuit, but he also responded to current affairs, nowhere more powerfully than in a poem called "Decease release" on the execution of Mary, Queen of Scots. The poem begins with a powerful description of the natural world:

> The pounded spice both tast and sent doth please
> In fading smoke the force doth incense shewe
> The perisht kernell springeth with encrease
> The lopped tree doth best and soonest growe.

As we move into the second stanza, these images are then applied to Mary, Queen of Scots herself:

> Gods spice I was and pounding was my due
> In fadinge breath my incense savored best

Death was the meane my kyrnell to renewe
By lopping shott I upp to heavenly rest.

It is worth remembering that Southwell was not simply exercising his wit, or poetic skill, in these verses. He knew full well that Mary's fate was likely to be his too. In a prayer he wrote while still a student in Rome, he asked God for a martyr's end: "For Thy sake allow me to be tortured, mutilated, scourged, slain and butchered. I refuse nothing. I will embrace all, I will endure all, not indeed I, dust and ashes as I am, but Thou, my Lord, in me." Just a few years after Mary's death he got his wish.

Southwell's life may have been cut short but, then as now, the blood of the martyrs was the seed of the Church. His life, death and poetry continue to inspire us today.

St John of the Cross
Poems (16th century)

St John of the Cross was a remarkable writer. A Doctor of the Church, mystic, and Carmelite friar, he is also widely regarded as one of the greatest Spanish poets of all time. As Martin D'Arcy, S.J., pointed out in his introduction to Roy Campbell's translations, "it would appear that poetry was more natural to him than prose." In fact, some of his most well-known mystical works, such as *The Dark Night* and the *Ascent of Mount Carmel*, started as commentaries on his poetry. His poetry was certainly not a decorative after-thought to his other work.

St John's topic was nothing less than the soul's mystical ascent to God, a journey that inevitably escapes the grasp of mere words, which is perhaps why he turned primarily to the music of poetry rather than to more earthbound prose. A wonderful example of his approach can be found in a poem with the unpromising title "Other verses with a divine meaning," in which he compares himself to a falcon chasing a divine quarry. Instead of swooping down on his prey, the soul's falcon rises higher and higher in his "amorous quest":

> The more I rose into the height
> More dazzled, blind, and lost I spun.
> The greatest conquest ever won
> I won in blindness, like the night.
> Because love urged me on my way
> I gave that mad, blind, reckless leap
> That soared me up so high and steep
> That in the end I seized my prey.

The soul in search of God is a commonplace notion but St John transforms it into something else entirely, with an extended metaphor that turns our usual view of the hunted and the hunter upside down. St John is most closely associated in the popular mind with the "dark night of the soul," but the repeated refrain ("Till in the end I seized my prey") reminds us that in his poetry the light of Christ finally sweeps away the night's dark.

Another poem that speaks of hope and love is "Verses written after an ecstasy of high exaltation." The repeated refrain in this work is "Toda sciencia trascendiendo" ("Transcending knowledge with my thought") and the theme of the poem is the relationship between knowledge, thought, and mystical experience:

> I entered in, I know not where,
> And I remained, though knowing naught,
> Transcending knowledge with my thought.

Swept up into the ecstasy of the knowledge of God, he finds that the usual categories and the usual words no longer seem to apply:

> So borne aloft, so drunken-reeling,
> So rapt was I, so swept away,
> Within the scope of sense or feeling
> My sense or feeling could not stay.
> And in my soul I felt, revealing,
> A sense that, though its sense was naught,
> Transcended knowledge with my thought.

This is not simply a poem about the inadequacy of words: it is rather a poem about the fullness of God and the fullness of the soul in God:

If you would ask, what is its essence—
This summit of all sense and knowing:
It comes from the Divinest Presence—
The sudden sense of him outflowing,
In His great clemency bestowing
The gift that leaves men knowing naught,
Yet passing knowledge with their thought.

If ever there was a poet who was caught up into the love and life of Christ, it was St John of the Cross. With the help of his poetry, we too can hope for the same.

Robin Hood and the Monk
(mid-15th century)

Robin Hood and the Monk is the earliest surviving tale of the outlaw, so what do find in this story that is missing from later retellings? First and foremost we discover that Robin longs to attend Mass and has a devotion to Our Lady:

> "Ye, on thing greves me," seid Robyn,
> "And does my hert mych woo:
> That I may not so solem day
> To mas nor matins goo.
> "Hit is a fourtnet and more," seid he,
> "Syn I my Savyour see;
> To day wil I to Notyngham," seid Robyn,
> "With the might of mylde Marye."

Attending Mass in Nottingham was clearly a risky business for an outlaw, but, missing the sight of his Lord in the Blessed Sacrament, Robin ignored the advice of Much the miller's son to take twelve outlaws with him and set out with only Little John for company. Unfortunately the two soon quarreled, leaving Robin to continue on his own. Knowing the risk, he prayed for protection:

> Whan Robyn came to Notynham,
> Sertenly withouten layn,
> He prayed to God and myld Mary
> To bring hym out save agayn.
> He gos in to Seynt Mary chirch,
> And knelyd down before the rode [the cross];
> Alle thatever were the church within
> Beheld wel Robyn Hode.

However, an avaricious monk who had previously been robbed of £100 promptly betrayed him to the sheriff and, despite putting up a brave fight, Robin was thrown into prison. This news prompted Little John to forget his anger and to remind the other outlaws of Robin's devotion to Our Lady:

> "He has servyd Oure Lady many a day,
> And yet wil, securely;
> Therfor I trust in hir specialy
> No wyckud deth shal he dye."

Together with Much the miller's son, Little John then ambushed the monk while he was on his way to London to tell the king the good news of Robin's arrest and, taking the monk's place, delivered the Sheriff of Nottingham's letters himself, explaining the original monk's absence by saying that he had died on the way. In a great comic twist, he returned to Nottingham with a letter from the king that commanded the sheriff to hand Robin over and this time explained the monk's absence by saying that the king was so pleased with him that he "has made hym abot of Westmynster."

Having drunk the sheriff's finest wine, Little John and Much the miller's son freed Robin during the night and brought him back in triumph to Sherwood Forest, where they celebrated their triumph:

> Whan his men saw hym hol and sounde,
> For soth they were fill fayne [glad].
> They filled in wyne and made hem glad,
> Under the levys smale,
> And yete pastes [ate pasties] of venison,
> That gode was with ale.

And so the tale ends with right restored, true religion confirmed, and Eden remembered. It is a miniature masterpiece that can take us right back to the legend's Catholic roots.

English Mystery Plays
(late 14th–late 16th century)

There are few more poignant reminders of the world we have lost than the pre-Reformation mystery plays. These dramas probably were originally performed on the Feast of Corpus Christi by different guilds that processed through cities such as York and Chester on elaborate pageant carts. As spectacles, they were hugely popular, so much so indeed that they survived the early years of the Reformation, albeit in an attenuated form, eventually being banned outright only in the middle years of Elizabeth I's reign.

As in the work of Sor Juana Inéz de la Cruz, these plays centered around the life, death, and resurrection of Christ as re-presented in the Sacrifice of the Mass, but they covered the whole of salvation history, starting with the fall of Lucifer and the creation of man and finishing with the Assumption and Coronation of Our Lady and Doomsday.

Some of these mystery plays have been revived or adapted in the twentieth century, with Benjamin Britten's *Noye's Fludde* being a notable example, but others have been almost entirely forgotten, especially the ones that fell foul of the Protestant reformers. A case in point is *The Harrowing of Hell*, which describes Christ's descent into Hell on Holy Saturday, a story that appeared in many different artistic forms until the early Protestants cast a disapproving eye on it.

The play begins with Jesus arriving at the Gates of Hell and then introduces Adam and Eve, Isaiah, Simeon, John the Baptist, and Moses, all of whom are waiting to be liberated by Christ. His arrival provokes a degree of panic among the devils, one of whom cries for help:

> Helpe, Belsabub, to bynde thes boyes!
> Such harrowe was never are herde in helle.
> [Help, Beelzebub, to bind these boys!
> Such an uproar was never heard in hell before.]

Beelzebub in turn summons further reinforcements but no one, least of all "Sir Sattanne" himself, is able to prevent Christ from breaking down the gates. Nonetheless, Satan still attempts to engage Christ in theological debate, casting doubt on his divine fatherhood and then on his right to remove Moses and the others from Hell. However, Christ triumphs in the debate, Satan "synke[s] in to helle pitte," and Christ is praised by Adam, Eve and the others before the play ends with them all being led out of Hell by St Michael.

Significantly in a play that points to the saving work of Christ, the last words go to Adam. Having brought sin into the world, he is redeemed by Christ, the second Adam, and so is now able to lead other redeemed souls (including, presumably, the citizens of York) in a paean of praise:

> To the, Lorde, be lovyng,
> That us has wonne fro waa;
> For solas will we syng
> *Laus tibi cum gloria.*
> [To you, Lord, be praise,
> Who has won us from woe;
> For solace will we sing
> Praise be to you with glory.]

Sir Gawain and the Green Knight
(late 14th century)

Sometimes stories develop a life of their own. They outlive the age in which they were written while remaining deeply rooted in it. The Robin Hood stories are good examples and so are the Arthurian legends. By the time the unknown author of *Sir Gawain and the Green Knight* wrote his story, the legend it related was already very old. In fact, as J.R.R. Tolkien once said in a masterful lecture, the poem "belongs to that literary kind which has deep roots in the past, deeper even than its author was aware." This historical depth really matters because, as Tolkien continued, behind "our poem stalk the figures of elder myth, and through the lines are heard the echoes of ancient cults, beliefs and symbols remote from the consciousness of an educated moralist (but also a poet) of the late fourteenth century. His story is not *about* those old things, but it receives part of its life, its vividness, its tension from them." Indeed, Tolkien argues, that is the way with all great fairy-stories.

Tolkien was acutely aware of the contemporary prejudice against fairy-stories, which is why he so often defended them (and wrote them), claiming that there is "indeed no better medium for moral teaching than the good fairy-story (by which I mean a real, deep-rooted tale, told as a tale, and not a thinly disguised moral allegory)." In that parenthetical comment you have a wonderful summary not only of *Sir Gawain and the Green Knight* but also of Chaucer's *Troilus and Criseyde*, Chrétien de Troyes' *Arthurian Romances*, and Tolkien's collected works.

Sir Gawain and the Green Knight is a deep-rooted tale, but it is also a deeply Christian tale. The action begins during the Christmas festivities at Camelot when a strange green man seated on a green horse bursts into the hall and throws down a challenge. Anyone may strike him with his axe if, a year and a day later, he is prepared to be struck himself at the knight's green chapel. Eager for adventure, King Arthur is about to take up the challenge when Sir Gawain intervenes to save him. Taking the axe, Gawain chops off the green giant's head only to see the man walk across the hall, pick it up, and leave the way he came.

True to his word, Sir Gawain sets off on his quest to find the green giant a year later and, after praying that he might be able to attend Mass in the morning, stumbles across a lonely castle where he is given refuge. In this longest section of the poem, Gawain is put to the test (though he does not realize it at the time), being tempted by the lady of the house while her husband is out hunting. Gawain manages to resist and sets out for the green chapel on the appointed day. In the depths of winter when the "snawe snitered ful snart" (the snow sleeted down sharply) and "mist mugged on the mor," he faces his final and most dreadful test. Finding the green knight, he presents his neck for the return blow and flinches just once as the knight prepares to kill him.

What happens next brings us to the emotional and moral core of this wonderful poem, but to say any more might discourage you from reading it for yourself, so I'm going to stop here and leave you, like Sir Gawain, to travel on alone.

The Cloud of Unknowing
(late 14th century)

Reading literature from the past can be a disconcerting experience because it challenges so much of what we take for granted. Take the opening of *The Cloud of Unknowing*, for example. After a prayer, the anonymous author sets out in no uncertain terms who is, and who is not, to read his book. There is absolutely no sense at all that he wants his book to be read by as many people as possible (or that he wants to sell as many copies as he can): *The Cloud of Unknowing* is intended only for the person who truly wants "to be a perfect follower of Christ" and who has prepared himself "for the contemplative life by means of virtuous active living." What is more, the reader is enjoined to give the book the attention it truly deserves: he must "take time to read it, speak of it, copy it, or hear it, all through." This may have been a challenge to readers in the fourteenth century: it is even more of a challenge today.

The unknown author makes it clear that anyone who wants to be a follower of Christ will inevitably enter a cloud of unknowing, a darkness between us and God. In searching for God, he tells us, we have to put aside everything but God himself. We tend to cling to our thoughts and feelings or God's gifts, but we should rather be content with God himself. So how do we put aside all that is not God so that we can lay hold of God alone? Through love. Love alone is the means by which we may pierce through the cloud of unknowing: "By love may He be getyn and holden; bot bi thought neither."

Reading this beautiful sentence, we are forced to face a

question I have so far side-stepped. If we are to read the best Catholic literature from across the world and across the ages, how far can we rely on translations? The simple answer is that we should read the originals if we can and make do with good translations if we cannot, but there are grey areas, like the world of fourteenth-century English literature. Some works from this time, such as *Pearl*, are difficult to understand without a translation, but other books, like *The Cloud of Unknowing* (or *The Clowde of Unknowyng*), are not only accessible but are clearly more powerful in the original. To illustrate this, let us look at two translations of the key line I quoted above. The first, in the Hodder Christian Classics edition, is "By love may he be sought and held, but not by thought," which has none of the resonance of the original. The second—the Penguin Classics edition—also falls flat in comparison with what the original author wrote: "By love he can be grasped and held, but by thought neither grasped nor held." As we all know from watching Shakespeare, engaging with earlier forms of our own language can be a challenge, but out of this challenge come great rewards.

There are many wonderful passages in *The Cloud of Unknowing*, but I will restrict myself to just two. The first comes in a chapter about how to obtain perfect meekness. The author encourages us "to swink and swete"—to work and sweat—"in all that thou canst and mayst, for to gete thee a trewe knowing and a felyng of thiself as thou arte. And then I trowe [believe] that sone after that thou schalt have a trewe knowing and felyng of God as He is." And the second sums up the message of the book as a whole: "yif thou wilt stonde and not falle, seese [cease] never in thin entent, bot bete evermore on this cloude of unknowing that is betwixt thee and thi God with a sharpe darte of longing love."

But don't rely on my inadequate summary. Do what the author asked: take "tyme to rede it, speke it, write it, or here it, al over."

Julian of Norwich
Revelations of Divine Love
(late 14th century)

In 1373, a 30-year-old woman who was lying seriously ill in bed at her home in Norwich received a series of revelations, or "showings" as she called them. We know her as Julian of Norwich because she later became an anchorite at the Church of St Julian in Norwich, but her name and virtually every detail about her life are completely unknown to us. This is no accident. Julian herself was determined to point attention away from herself towards God, writing: "And therefore I beg you all for God's sake and advise you for your own advantage that you stop paying attention to the poor, worldly, sinful creature to whom this vision was shown, and eagerly, attentively, lovingly and humbly contemplate God, who in his gracious love and in his eternal goodness wanted the vision to be generally known to comfort us all."

What was this vision? It was a vision of love. A profound, all-enveloping, deeply mysterious love that Julian spent the rest of her life contemplating. That is why there are two versions of the Revelations of Divine Love, a shorter one and a much longer one produced years later when she had a more profound understanding of the showings that had been given to her. However, even in later life, she realized that the full glorious enormity of what she had seen could not be adequately captured in words. In fact, as she explained herself, her showings were never solely linguistic. She received them in three distinct ways: "by bodily sight, by words formed in my understanding, and by spiritual sight."

The most famous of the messages she received goes: "Sin is befitting, but all shall be well, and all shall be well, and all manner of things shall be well," though the first phrase is often omitted when the passage is quoted. This is unfortunate, for the sentence was a response to her question about why God had not prevented the beginning of sin, and the answer was one she tried to fathom for the rest of her life.

Julian was clearly a well-informed and well-educated woman, though she may not have received a formal education as we understand it today. Her writings are often very beautiful. Take this description of Julian's "soul in the middle of [her] heart," for example: "I saw the soul as large as if it were an endless world and as if it were a holy kingdom; and from the properties in it I understood that it is a glorious city. In the center of that city sits our Lord Jesus, God and man, a handsome person and of great stature, the highest bishop, the most imposing king, the most glorious Lord; and I saw him dressed imposingly and gloriously. He sits in the soul, in the very center, in peace and rest."

Another fascinating example is the parable of the lord and his servant. After being sent on a mission by his lord, the servant fell into a slough in his eagerness and was so badly hurt that he could not get out. Like all parables, this one appears very simple, but it took Julian nearly twenty years before she understood it fully. At first sight the servant seemed to represent Adam (who represents all mankind), with his falling into the slough representing the Fall, but, as Julian sought clarity, she realized that the servant was also Christ:

> When Adam fell, God's son fell; because of the true union made in heaven, God's son could not leave Adam, for by Adam I understand all men. Adam fell from life to death into the valley of this wretched world, and after that into

hell. God's son fell with Adam into the valley of the Virgin's womb (and she was the fairest daughter of Adam), in order to free Adam from guilt in heaven and in earth; and with his great power he fetched him out of hell.

It is a remarkable interpretation of a remarkable vision that demanded the years of thought and prayer that Julian gave to it. The fourteenth century was a remarkable era for Catholic literature in England and, though Julian would not have said so herself, her book was a wonderful contribution to that wonderful age.

Pearl
(late 14th century)

We are sometimes told that before the development of modern medicine people had a different attitude towards children from the one we have today. The argument goes that when child mortality rates were high, parents simply couldn't allow themselves to feel too deeply about their children. This wonderful Middle English poem suggests that such a view is very wide of the mark.

At the start of the poem the anonymous speaker loses a precious pearl in a garden and, overwhelmed by grief, falls asleep on the grass. In his dream he finds himself in a beautiful place where leaves shimmer as if made of silver and where the banks of the stream are covered with pearls rather than stones. On the far side of the stream he sees a beautiful young woman wearing a crown. When she tells him that she has become a bride of Christ and a queen of heaven, he recognizes her as his pearl, his daughter who died before her second birthday.

What follows is a remarkable conversation across the uncrossable stream, during which the daughter consoles the father, convincing him that, despite her extreme youth, she has been saved by God's grace and justified in baptism. She reminds him of the parable about the pearl of great price, explaining that it is the pearl she now wears on her breast. The longing of the father and the radiance of the daughter in heaven are described in beautifully complex poetry, with the result that, by the end of the poem, both the father and we, the readers, are reconciled to the death of his child. The sorrow has certainly not disappeared but the knowledge that she is not just safe but exalted in heaven is enough to make the pain bearable. Seen in the glorious light of heaven, the suffering the father experiences on earth no longer looks quite the same as it did at the beginning of the poem.

Pearl is a great poem in its own right but it is worth reading for other reasons too. We are beginning to find connections as we work our way back in time on our journey through Catholic literature. None of these works exists in isolation: looking backwards, *Pearl* draws on the Sacred Scriptures, Dante's *Divine Comedy*, and other works; looking forwards, it inspired later writers such as J. R. R. Tolkien, whose description of the hobbits' arrival at Lothlórien in *The Lord of the Rings* was clearly inspired by the earlier poem.

Tradition is often misunderstood. It can be seen as nothing more than naïve nostalgia, but it makes much more sense to think of tradition working both forwards and backwards in time. *The Lord of the Rings* can lead us to *Pearl*, which, in turn, can enhance our reading of Tolkien's great work. And both can point us beyond literature to the source of beauty, truth, and goodness, which is what their authors would have wanted.

Blessed Jacobus de Voragine
The Golden Legend (mid-13th century)

The village sign of Mayfield in East Sussex is worth a close look. Perched beneath the apex, two figures are pulling what appears to be a piece of wood from either end. On closer inspection, the observer can see that the figures depict a monk and the devil, and that the piece of wood is in fact a pair of tongs, whose sharp end is attached to the devil's nose. What we have here is St Dunstan, a tenth-century archbishop of Canterbury who was once visited by the devil while he worked at his forge, and what happened next was described in William Caxton's edition of *The Golden Legend*:

> And on a time as he sat at his work his heart was on Jesu Christ, his mouth occupied with holy prayers, and his hands busy on his work. But the devil, which ever had great envy at him, came to him in an eventide in the likeness of a woman, as he was busy to make a chalice, and with smiling said that she had great things to tell him, and then he bade her say what she would, and then she began to tell him many nice trifles, and no manner virtue therein, and then he supposed that she was a wicked spirit, and anon caught her by the nose with a pair of tongs of iron, burning hot, and then the devil began to roar and cry, and fast drew away, but S. Dunstan held fast till it was far within the night, and then let her go, and the fiend departed with a horrible noise and cry, and said, that all the people might hear: Alas! what shame hath this carle done to me, how may I best quit him again? But never after the devil had lust to tempt him in that craft.

Though neither this story nor St Dunstan himself featured in Jacobus de Voragine's *The Golden Legend*, such was the popularity of his book that it was soon translated into many different languages and, as often as not, supplemented with local legends like this one. However, if we look at the original version, we find that Voragine's approach was very similar to that adopted by Caxton and others. When describing the death of St Paul the Apostle, for example, he told the story of Plautilla, one of the apostle's followers. Paul asked her for a handkerchief with which to bind his eyes before he was beheaded, promising that he would return it later:

> And when she had delivered it to him, the butchers scorned her, saying: Why hast thou delivered to this enchanter so precious a cloth for to lose it? Then, when he came to the place of his passion, he turned him toward the east, holding his hands up to heaven right long, with tears praying in his own language and thanking our Lord, and after that bade his brethren farewell, and bound his eyes himself with the keverchief of Plautilla, and kneeling down on both knees, stretched forth his neck, and so was beheaded. And as soon as the head was from the body, it said: Jesus Christus! which had been to Jesus or Christus, or both, fifty times. From his wound sprang out milk into the clothes of the knight, and afterward flowed out blood. In the air was a great shining light, and from the body came a much sweet odour.... [He then] took the keverchief, and unbound his eyes, and gathered up his own blood, and put it therein and delivered [it] to the woman.

The Golden Legend is full of miraculous events like these, but it would be wrong to think of it as merely a collection of tall tales from a more credulous age. What Voragine actually provided in *The Golden Legend* was a manual for preachers structured around the liturgical year: a compendium of saints' lives as well as lots of information about doctrine and the liturgy.

The stories were so vivid that the book soon reached a much wider audience and was adapted as it traveled and was translated. However, we should not forget the book's liturgical roots. For many hundreds of years Catholic literature was not divorced from the wider life of the Church but was an integral part of it. Its subject matter, its style and even its structure was shaped by the Scriptures, the liturgy, and the Church year. This can make some early Christian writing feel rather strange to a modern reader, but the good news is that this unfamiliarity can be the path that leads us back to an understanding, and an imaginative appreciation, of an age that was open to the Faith in a way ours sadly no longer is. We should not lose ourselves in the past, wishing that modernity had never crept up on us, but neither should we forget that pre-modern literature still has a great deal to offer us—including *The Golden Legend* and its glorious collection of stories.

Dante Alighieri
The Divine Comedy (c. 1320)

One of the greatest poems of all times, Dante's description of an ascent through Hell and Purgatory into Paradise was written in the very first years of the fourteenth century but remains highly readable and extremely moving today. The boldness of Dante's vision and the breadth of his achievement put the limited ambition of most modern novels to shame.

The Divine Comedy is not a comedy in the modern sense of the word but a journey upwards to God. That is why the poem begins on earth with the poet lost in a wood at the mid-point of his life. Needing a guide to help him find his way, he meets Virgil, whose epic poem, the *Aeneid*, also contains a journey to the underworld that was itself inspired by Odysseus' descent into the place of the dead in Homer's *Odyssey*. Needing help, it was natural for him to turn to the great writers of the classical past. However, as a Christian, Dante knew what Virgil and Homer only dimly sensed, which is why his poem draws on the full riches of the Church's teaching about the afterlife, taking us far beyond what the pagan poets could describe. Virgil could get him started on his journey but could never take him to the final destination. In one sense, *The Divine Comedy* depends upon the greatest books of the classical world, but in another sense it completes them.

Virgil is a wonderful guide but, as a pagan, he is unable to take Dante all the way to Heaven. It is Beatrice, Dante's poetic muse, who leads him upwards, his human love for her a sacramental step on the way to the purified love he will experience only in Paradise. Indeed, what is most striking about his experience of Paradise is how dependent he is, as a sinful, mortal man, upon Beatrice. It is his love for her that makes the experience of Paradise possible. By looking at her, he is himself changed.

Another aspect of Paradise that might surprise contemporary readers—since Paradise is not a place that is ever considered with any degree of seriousness in modern fiction—is just how dynamic it is. As Dante ascends through each sphere his experience changes. He meets many saints, but what matters most in the poem is not the numbers but the ways in which these encounters change in nature and intensity. For example, towards the end of his epic journey, Beatrice says that if she were to smile at him he would be burnt to ashes. She is still Beatrice but, as a saint in Heaven, she is immeasurably more powerful (and more herself) than she ever was on earth. We might well ask how Dante, who is acutely aware of his sinful nature, can describe what is, by definition, indescribable. The answer is that he can't. Just as Tolkien held back from describing Paradise in *Leaf by Niggle* and just as the *Pearl* poet pointed out that no one can possibly describe the richness and happiness of Heaven, so too does Dante tell us that what he has seen in Paradise has faded from his memory, leaving him and us with only an inkling of its glories. What is beyond human comprehension must remain beyond words. Or, to put it another way, even the greatest of poems can only point us towards the greatest of visions.

St Thomas Aquinas
Corpus Christi Hymns (1264)

On August 11, 1264, Pope Urban IV issued the Papal Bull *Transiturus de hoc mundo*, which instituted the feast of Corpus Christi so that we might more suitably celebrate the "saving memorial in which we recall with gratitude the memory of our redemption, in which we are withdrawn from evil and strengthened in good and go forward to an increase of virtues and graces, in which we really go forward through the bodily presence of the Savior himself." Such a great feast required a suitable liturgy, which is why Pope Urban turned to Thomas Aquinas for help.

Among the hymns that St Thomas composed for the Corpus Christi Office were the *Pange lingua* (which begins "Sing, my tongue, the Savior's glory" and contains the *Tantum ergo* that is now sung at Benediction), the *Sacris solemniis* (which contains the *Panis angelicus*), and the *Lauda Sion*. These remarkable hymns are a wonderful combination of acute theological insight, intense devotion, and great poetic skill.

St Thomas also wrote the *Adoro te devote*, which seems to have been composed as a private prayer to be recited silently during Mass. Like the hymns that St Thomas wrote for the Corpus Christi Office, the *Adoro te devote* has been translated many times, but perhaps the finest translation came from Gerard Manley Hopkins, whose poetry we have already seen:

Godhead here in hiding, whom I do adore,
Masked by these bare shadows, shape and nothing more,

See, Lord, at thy service low lies here a heart
Lost, all lost in wonder at the God thou art.

Seeing, touching, tasting are in thee deceived;
How says trusty hearing? That shall be believed:
What God's Son has told me, take for truth I do;
Truth himself speaks truly or there's nothing true.

Both the original prayer and the translation are superb poems, with Hopkins' translation of Aquinas's wonderful "Nihil veritatis verbo verius" being particularly effective: "Truth himself speaks truly or there's nothing true." As aids to devotion during the Mass, they may well be unsurpassed; but there is another reason why we might want to consider the poetry that was created for the feast of Corpus Christi in our survey of Catholic literature. Writing about the work of David Jones, Jean Ward has drawn attention to what she calls a "poetics of hidden presence." Such a notion, which is drawn from Eucharistic theology, can be applied not just to David Jones but to the work of all Catholic writers. We have already seen the importance of "presence" to Les Murray and have briefly touched on "the operation of divine grace" in the novels of Evelyn Waugh, but a similar reading could be given of all the authors represented in this book. There is a hidden presence in all Catholic literature; words are both important and terribly unimportant; or, to put it another way, words gain significance only when they point to the Word Himself. This is a great mystery, as St Thomas knew, so if we are looking for a way into the great tradition of Catholic literature we should certainly not neglect the great poetry that Pope Urban IV commissioned in 1264.

Snorri Sturluson
Egil's Saga
(early 13th century)

We have probably all read retellings of the Norse myths in which the lives of Odin, Thor, Baldr and other gods are recounted. Theirs is a pagan world that has little if anything to do with the Christian world that displaced it. But if we return to the earliest written accounts of these tales we find quite a different picture. Snorri Sturluson's *Edda*, for example, begins not with the gods but with God. In fact, one of the tasks the author sets himself is to explain how paganism could have developed. He explains that "as time passed mankind became diverse: some were good and orthodox in faith, but many more turned aside to follow the lusts of the world and neglected God's commandments." These men, who retained only a dim memory of the one true God, still tried to make sense of the world in which they found themselves, though they lacked divine inspiration. As a consequence, the religions they created for themselves were "a rational but misguided groping towards the truth," as Anthony Faulkes puts it.

But there is another reason why Snorri Sturluson and others were interested in the lives and stories of their pagan forefathers, as J. R. R. Tolkien explained in his masterly essay "Beowulf: The Monsters and the Critics." According to Tolkien, *Beowulf* was written

> from a pregnant moment of poise, looking back into the pit, by a man learned in old tales who was struggling, as it were, to get a general view of them all, perceiving their

common tragedy of inevitable ruin, and yet feeling this more *poetically* because he was himself removed from the direct presence of its despair.

It is with these key facts in mind that we need to read *Egil's Saga*, which was probably written by Snorri Sturluson and was certainly written by a Christian Icelander about the largely pre-Christian Nordic past. The saga is an often highly violent account that seems far removed from any Christian concerns. To give just one example, when he was just seven years old, Egil took revenge on Grim, a boy who had humiliated him during a game:

> Thord handed Egil an axe he had been holding, a common type of weapon in those days. They walked over to where the boys were playing their game. Grim had caught the ball and was running with the other boys chasing him. Egil ran up to Grim and drove the axe into his head, right through to the brain. Then Egil and Thord walked away to their people.

While such an act of revenge may have made sense in a pagan, warrior society, it seems entirely out of place in a book written by a Christian. The problem is compounded by the style of the work. Sagas (and, indeed, most pre-modern literature) focus on external actions rather than on interior states, leaving the reader to make his or her own judgments about the characters and their actions. Being left to our own devices can be unsettling, but Snorri's attitude to the pre-Christian Icelanders can be deduced from the very last pages of the book, which take us from the pre-Christian world to the very different world of Christian Iceland:

> Thorstein, Egil's son, was baptized when Christianity came to Iceland and he had a church built at Borg. He was

a devout and orderly man. He grew to an old age, died of illness and was buried at Borg in the church he had built there.

To grow to old age and die of illness would have been a remarkable achievement for any pagan Viking. Being buried in the church he had built took this transformation to another level. This may be Egil's *Saga*, but it is Thorstein and the Christian worldview he represents that ultimately triumph.

St Hildegard of Bingen
Symphonia armonie celestium revelationem (1175)

When Benedict XVI proclaimed St Hildegard of Bingen a Doctor of the Universal Church in 2012, he drew attention to her extremely wide-ranging contribution to Church and society, reminding us that the "profound spirituality of her writings had a significant influence both on the faithful and on important figures of her time and brought about an incisive renewal of theology, liturgy, natural sciences and music."

Hildegard recorded the visions that she had received from childhood onwards in books such as the *Liber Divinorum Opera* and the *Scivias*, which concludes with a morality play that she later developed into the *Ordo Virtutum* (the Play of Virtues). She also wrote medical textbooks, created what she called a *Lingua Ignota* ("an unknown language"), and was a fine composer. In fact, her visions were as much aural as visual, sometimes appearing as "a sound like the voice of a multitude singing in harmony, in praise of the celestial hierarchy," as she wrote in the *Scivias*. Her liturgical compositions were collected in the *Symphonia armonie celestium revelationem*, which contains some wonderful poetry as well as some glorious music.

The first responsory in the *Symphonia* draws on the style of the Psalms and is remarkable for its controlled use of language:

> O vis eternitatis
> que omnia ordinasti in corde tuo,

per Verbum tuum omnia creata sunt
sicut voluisti,
et ipsum Verbum tuum
induit carnem
in formatione illa
que educta est de Adam,

Et sic indumenta ipsius
a maximo dolore
abstersa sunt.

[O strength of eternity,
you who ordered all things in your heart,
by your Word all were created
as you wished,
and your Word himself
put on flesh
in that form
which was taken from Adam.

And thus his garments were cleansed
from the greatest pain.]

But not all St Hildegard's compositions were in Latin. She
wrote one of them in her *lingua ignota*, which only deepens
the mystery surrounding the language:

O orzchis Ecclesia,
armis divinis precincta
et iacincto ornata,
tu es caldemia stigmatum loifolum
et urbs scientiarum.
O, o, tu es etiam crizanta
in alto sono
et es chorzta gemma.

[O measureless Church,
girded with divine arms
and adorned with jacinth,
you are the fragrance of the wounds of nations
and the city of sciences.
O, O, and you are anointed
amid noble sound,
and you are a sparkling gem.]

Whatever the reason for this rich linguistic response to the measureless Church, we, and the many who are rediscovering Hildegard's music, can certainly be grateful for it. Her work was the dazzling product of a wide-ranging intellect and acute spiritual insight, but when we hear these compositions as they were meant to be heard, in the context of worship, it is not St Hildegard's talent that we focus on but the God whom she worshipped so devoutly and resolutely throughout her amazing life.

Chrétien de Troyes
Arthurian Romances (late 12th century)

I was taken aback when I first came across the list of the Knights of the Round Table in Chrétien de Troyes' Arthurian romances. Chrétien introduces us to Gornemant of Gohort, the Fair Coward, the Ugly Hero, Meliant de Liz, Mauduit the Wise, Dodinel the Wildman, Gaudelu, Yvain the Valiant, Yvain the Bastard, Blioberis, Caradué Shortarm, Caveron de Roberdic, the son of King Quenedic, the youth of Quintareus, Yder of the Sorrowful Mountain, Galeriet, Kay of Estral, Amauguin, Galet the Bald, Girflet son of Do, Taulas, Loholt, Sagremor the Unruly, Bedoier the constable ("who knew much of chess and backgammon"), Bravaïn, King Lot, and Galegantin.

It is true that he also mentions Gawain, Lancelot of the Lake, and Tristan, but even so the company is very unfamiliar, despite the fact that the Arthurian legends are so deeply embedded in our cultural memory. That his list of knights should be so unfamiliar is surprising, because Chrétien created the Arthurian legends as we know them today. He was the first to describe Guinevere's affair with Lancelot, the first to mention Camelot, and the first to write about the Grail legend. All these stories have passed into the mainstream, which makes the oblivion into which some of his other romances have sunk all the more baffling.

This becomes especially clear when we look at his first romance, *Erec and Enide*, which starts not with the sword in the stone, nor with Merlin, nor with Camelot, but with Erec, son of Lac. There are several striking features to this tale, the most important of which is its theme: marital love.

Setting off from Cardigan Castle (where Arthur's court is), Erec meets and falls in love with Enide. He brings her back to the court, where they are married and begin a life of marital bliss. However, Erec soon wonders how he can serve both honor (*armes*) and love (*armors*). Thus his adventures begin. Or rather, their adventures, because Eric leaves the safety of the court accompanied by his wife rather than by other knights. They are to be tested together.

Another striking feature of the romance, which is developed further in the later romances, is the way it is grounded in the liturgical year and in liturgical practice. The narrator often frames their journey with references to the monastic hours: "They entered a forest and did not stop until the hour of prime" is a typical comment. More significantly, *Erec and Enide* begins "on Easter day" and ends with a Coronation Mass on Christmas day. Chrétien drew from, and relied upon, a rich liturgical setting to shape and redeem the action of the stories.

All of this helps us make sense of Chrétien's opening comment in *Erec and Enide*, where he explained the role of the Catholic writer:

> And so Chrétien de Troyes says that it is reasonable for everyone to think and strive in every way to speak well and to teach well, and from a tale of adventure he draws a beautifully ordered composition that clearly proves that a man does not act intelligently if he does not give free rein to his knowledge for as long as God gives him the grace to do so.

The story is beautifully ordered, not simply as a composition by a master storyteller, but also as a product of a deeply Catholic imagination. It is ordered to God and shaped by the liturgical life of the Church. In that respect, it is quite typical of a great deal of pre-Reformation literature. In that respect, it can seem quite distant to us. There is a bridge that needs to be crossed when it comes to pre-modern literature, but if we are bold enough to do so we will find that the rewards are very great indeed.

The Song of Roland
(late 11th century)

The Song of Roland has been called the most ancient and most beautiful of the *chansons de geste*, the epic tales sung by traveling minstrels called jongleurs. About a hundred of these tales, composed between the eleventh and fourteenth centuries, survive to this day but *The Song of Roland* is one of the finest. Though primarily associated with France, it is entirely possible that it was created in England; we know that the story of Roland's tragic death at Roncevaux was a popular one and that it was sung to the Norman invaders before the Battle of Hastings, but who wrote the version that has come down to us is still something of a mystery.

The Song of Roland is based on real events—an attack on Charlemagne's rearguard as he returned from a military campaign in Spain in 778—but the poetic version presents a version of the story that seemed more pertinent to the time in which it was written, Charlemagne's enemy being the Muslims (or "pagans" as they are usually called in the poem) who then controlled much of Spain rather than the Basques who may actually have attacked his troops as they made their way back across the Alps. However, though the poem tells a story of war and heroism, it does not present an entirely triumphalist account of a Christian victory over the Islamic enemy: the poem centers around the tragic death of Roland, who is betrayed by one of his own side, and it ends on a curiously ambivalent note. Having had the defeated Muslim king baptized, Charlemagne retires to his chamber where he is visited by the Archangel Gabriel:

Saint Gabriel came to him in God's name:
"Charles, summon your imperial armies.
You will invade the land of Bire,
And help King Vivien in Imphe,
The city which the pagans have besieged.
The Christians call upon you and cry out for you."
The emperor had no wish to go.
"God," said the king, "how wearisome my life is!"
He weeps and tugs at his white beard.

Downbeat as this ending may be, we have been prepared for it by earlier events. When ambushed in a narrow pass, Roland refuses to blow on his horn (his "olifant"), fearing to lose his good name. Fighting on against great odds, he only blows his horn when it is clear that he is going to die. He summons Charlemagne not so that he will be saved but so that the emperor will be able to avenge his faithful soldiers' deaths. It is his horn rather than his sword, Durendal, that becomes a great national emblem, recalling an act of great sacrifice as well as one of great heroism. It is Roland's noble death rather than Charlemagne's victory that resonates through the years.

The Dream of the Rood
(*c.* 8th century)

Before the word "cross" entered the English language, the word for the cross on which Jesus died was "rood." It was a very familiar word in Old English, not least because St Helena's discovery of the true cross in the fourth century led to a widespread devotion, which inevitably found its way into literature.

An example of this interest is *Elene*, Cynewulf's long poem about St Helena's pilgrimage to the Holy Land. The poem begins with a stirring, though anachronistic, account of the events that preceded the Battle of the Milvian Bridge; on the night before the battle the Emperor Constantine (according to the poem) was given a vision by an angel: "He beheld the radiant Tree of glory above the dome of clouds, bright with gems, adorned with gold; its jewels gleamed." After winning the battle and converting to Christianity, he encouraged his mother in her quest to find the true cross, which eventually she did. It is a story which continued to fascinate Catholic authors, with Evelyn Waugh writing a particularly fine novel about St Helena a thousand years after Cynewulf's poem.

The greatest poem to have been written about the cross in the Anglo-Saxon era was *The Dream of the Rood*, which, like *Pearl*, begins with a dream. In his sleep the poet sees "a wondrous tree soaring into the air, surrounded by light." Clearly this is no ordinary tree: in fact, it is the cross of Christ that is now "entirely cased in gold" with beautiful jewels at its foot. The glorified cross is guarded by angels but still shows the signs of its agony, having bloodstains down its right side.

The poet lies on his bed for a long time, sadly contemplating the sight.

But the poem doesn't end there. What makes this poem remarkable is what happens next. The cross begins to speak, telling the poet how it was felled at the edge of the forest, seized by his enemies and set up on a hill. The language is the language of war, and Christ, when he enters the poem, is described as a young warrior.

The cross wants to bow down before him but knows it has to stand firm, because Christ too is described as a warrior who could have felled all his foes had he chosen to do so. The cross knows that its task is quite different: to stand by and hold up his king, to endure the horrors of battle and, finally, emerging triumphant, to "heal all those who stand in awe of me."

After encouraging its hearers to carry "the best of all signs" at their breast and to "search for a kingdom far beyond the frontiers of this world," the cross falls silent and we return to the poet, who has now cast off his earlier sadness and become eager and lighthearted as he meditates on the cross and looks forward to escaping this "fleeting life" and finding "the home of joy and happiness where the people of God are seated at the feast in eternal bliss." Drawn out of himself through contemplation of the cross, he is able to return strengthened, though not unchanged, to the everyday world.

St Bede
Ecclesiastical History of the English People (c. 731)

In 1899 the Venerable Bede was declared a Doctor of the Church. A man who had never held high office was now officially one of the Church's great teachers. Why was a mere historian so highly regarded by Pope Leo XIII? To answer that question we need to say that Bede was not just a historian. He wrote many Bible commentaries and was particularly interested in time, writing two important books on the subject.

But it is true that his greatest work was his *Ecclesiastical History of the English People*, a book we will only get to grips with if we understand that, for Bede, history was much more than a bare record of events. "If history records good things of good men," he wrote, "the thoughtful hearer is encouraged to imitate what is good: or if it records evil of wicked men, the devout, religious listener or reader is encouraged to avoid all that is sinful and perverse and to follow what he knows to be good and pleasing to God."

Such an approach might seem surprising in the twenty-first century. We assume that history should be objective or neutral. But it never is. Historians select material according to their own priorities and beliefs. Bede did the same, only his priorities and beliefs were different from the ones held by most modern historians.

When, for example, he wrote the famous passage about St Gregory the Great first seeing English slaves in the Roman marketplace, he was not simply showing off the pope's verbal dexterity (the Angles, who had angelic faces, would become co-heirs with the angels in heaven, St Gregory said). He was also making a point about who was responsible for the evangelization of the English. For Bede it was important to emphasize that it was primarily St Gregory rather than St Augustine of Canterbury or St Aidan who was the Apostle of the English. The English were converted because the pope reached out to them from Rome.

Though he probably never set foot outside Northumbria, Bede was certainly not a parochial figure. As a faithful historian, he wanted to show that the English Church was part of the universal Church whose center on earth was Rome. England's first historian knew that England could only be understood in its Roman context.

If the English Church needed to be understood in its Roman context, then all of history needed to be seen in a broader context too. It needed to be seen in the light of eternity, as we can see in one of Bede's most famous stories.

When Edwin, the King of Northumbria, was trying to decide whether to convert to Christianity, he held a council to decide the question. "When we compare the present life of man on earth with that time of which we have no knowledge," one of his men told him, "it seems to me like the swift flight of a single sparrow through the banqueting-hall where you are sitting at dinner on a winter's day with your thegns and counsellors. In the midst there is a comforting fire to warm the hall; outside, the storms of winter rain or snow are raging. This sparrow flies swiftly in through one door of the hall, and out through another. While he is inside, he is safe from the winter storms; but after a few moments of comfort, he vanishes from sight into the wintry world from which he came. Even so, man appears on earth for a little while; but of what went before this life or of what follows, we know nothing. Therefore, if this new teaching has brought us any more certain knowledge, it seems only right that we should follow it." Like Bede, Edwin's advisor knew that life is brief and that eternity is what really matters.

But, as every monk also knows, eternity has already broken into this world. Bede saw the history of the English people as having been caught up into the events of salvation history. That is why he did not shy away from including healings and other miracles in his account of the historical development of the English people. The wonders that were described in the Acts of the Apostles had not just stopped, he believed; the Holy Spirit continued to work in human history.

As a historian of the English Bede had no equals. He created a sense of what it meant to be English before England existed as a country, and he created a model of faithful scholarship that inspired writers, missionaries, and popes for years after his death. For all these reasons, he is well worth reading today.

St Isidore of Seville
Etymologies (636)

Born into a notable Christian family around 560, St Isidore was educated by his brother, Leander, who later became Bishop of Seville and who was a friend of St Gregory the Great, as well as a confidant of kings and princes in Visigothic Spain. After Leander's death, Isidore was also chosen as Bishop of Seville, but his elevation to the episcopate did not put an end to his writing career. He continued to produce many different books, ranging from volumes on the liturgy to a history of the Vandals.

The *Etymologies* is by far the best known of these books. In fact, it has recently been suggested that "it was arguably the most influential book, after the Bible, in the learned world of the Latin West for nearly a thousand years." It was quoted by William Langland, Geoffrey Chaucer and Blessed Jacobus de Voragine, while Dante went one step further by writing about Isidore himself in his *Paradiso*.

So what sort of book is the *Etymologies*? It is a difficult book to categorize but, if we are to use modern categories, we might say that it falls somewhere between an encyclopedia and an etymological dictionary. In an age in which intellectual errors like Arianism were causing huge damage to the Church, Isidore believed that the educated elite needed a comprehensive guide to see them through life.

The *Etymologies* contains chapters on everything from buildings and fields to the cosmos and its parts. It ranges from descriptions of God, angels, and the saints to a chapter on mathematics, music and astronomy. There are also some wonderful descriptions of animals, including a passage about the elephant (which can be found in between accounts of the rhinoceros and the griffin). St Isidore tells us not only that elephants live for three hundred years and gestate for two years, but also that they have great intellects and a wonderful memory. He writes that they run away from mice, "mate facing away from each other," and give birth in water or on islands because of their fear of snakes, which are capable of killing them with their coils. He also explains that:

> These animals were called "Lucan cows" by the ancient Romans; "cows" because they had seen no animal larger than a cow, and "Lucan" because it was in Lucania that Pyrrhus first set them against the Romans in battle. This kind of animal is suited to warfare, for the Persians and Indians, having set wooden towers on them, attack with javelins as if from a rampart.

This account may not be scientifically accurate but it might sound familiar. When Tolkien was writing about the oliphaunt in *The Lord of the Rings* he drew on the Book of Maccabees and on the work of St Aelfric, who, in turn, obtained much of his description from the *Etymologies*. If we follow the history of Catholic literature with determination, we will discover some very surprising connections.

St John Chrysostom
Homilies (late 4th/early 5th century)

We tend to define literature very narrowly today, thinking only of novels, poetry and plays, but if we look back in time we find that our forebears worked with a much wider conception of literature. We have already seen examples of hymns, saints' lives, and histories, so it is now time to look at some homilies from the great fifth-century theologian and bishop, St John Chrysostom.

Having been educated in the pagan classics, St John became a monk and was soon sought after as an astute interpreter of the Sacred Scriptures. Chrysostom means "golden-mouthed" in Greek and was a reference to St John's rhetorical skills, but during his time as a priest in Antioch and as bishop in Constantinople he also became widely known for his pastoral understanding. He drew on all these experiences in his homilies, which remain inspiring today. His homilies on St Paul's Epistle to the Ephesians, for instance, are well worth reading for the acute insights they provide into marriage and family life, with his homily on Ephesians 6: 1–4 sounding a very modern note:

> It is necessary for everyone to know Scriptural teachings, and this is especially true for children. Even at their age they are exposed to all sorts of folly and bad examples from popular entertainments. Our children need remedies for all these things! We are so concerned with our children's schooling; if only we were equally zealous in bringing them up in the discipline and instruction of the Lord!

And in another passage he explains the practical benefits of following St Paul's teaching:

> Concern for spiritual things will unite the family. Do you want your child to be obedient? Then from the beginning bring him up in the discipline and instruction of the Lord. Don't think that it isn't necessary for a child to listen to the Scriptures; the first thing he will hear from them will be, "Honor your father and your mother," and immediately you will begin to reap your reward.

St John was an incredibly practical writer. It is easy to be daunted by the Fathers of the Church, convincing ourselves that their work will be impenetrable and inaccessible, but the truth is that, from St Augustine's account of his childhood crimes in the *Confessions* to St John Chrysostom's pastoral advice, their work is grounded in reality and so is often readily accessible. To give just one more example, St John starts his homily on Ephesians 6:1–4 by saying:

> Listen to what [St Paul] says: "Children, obey your parents in the Lord, for this is the first commandment with a promise." He will not speak here about Christ, or other lofty subjects, but will direct his words to young minds; that is also why this passage is very short, since children have a short span of attention.

In that respect at least, little has changed between the fifth century and today! From his earliest days as a monk, St John was known as a great orator and preacher; but, as these homilies reveal, part of his greatness lay in his ability to write simply and clearly, adapting his message to his audience. That is one reason why his work has stood the test of time.

St Augustine
Confessions (397–398)

The foundational book for all Christian literature is clearly the Bible, but if any other book comes close it is St Augustine's *Confessions*. This remarkable work is sometimes described as the first autobiography, but in truth it is a much more complex book than that. Written at the very end of the fourth century, the *Confessions* is as much an extended prayer as an autobiography, but even that description is misleading, for the prayer that runs through the thirteen sections of the book is one that reveals the full range of St Augustine's astounding intellect. It is not so much that he wrestles with God as that he wrestles with his own understanding of God and his own understanding of himself in the light of his relationship with God. It is quite different from any modern autobiography.

The *Confessions* are so readable partly because St Augustine writes with incredible honesty about his own struggles and desires. He writes about his sins, his early heresies, the terrible way he treated his mother, and many other issues that most people would gloss over, before also writing about the process of his conversion. And he writes about all these mistakes without a trace of self-pity, self-glorification or self-indulgence. In fact, since he is deeply aware of his own sinfulness, he knows how difficult it is to plumb the depths of his own heart, which means that he constantly probes and questions his own life and work. As a result, even the most well-known passages—for example, the story about his youthful theft of some pears—and the most well-known lines—"You have made us for Yourself and our hearts are restless until they rest in You"—are more complex than they might at first appear. St Augustine never tells anecdotes for their own sake: he uses the story of his life as a way of probing the workings of God.

When I studied the *Confessions* at university, we looked at only the first nine books, the ones that are most obviously autobiographical. But Augustine knew what he was doing: the last four books are not simply an appendix to the main work but address hugely important questions. In attempting to make sense of the operation of divine grace in his own life, Augustine is taken away from himself to ponder profound questions about time, memory, and the creation of the world, finishing with a contemplation of the relationship between God's work and God's rest:

> In that eternal Sabbath you will rest in us, just as now you work in us. The rest that we shall enjoy will be yours, just as the work that we now do is your work done through us. But you, O Lord, are eternally at work and eternally at rest. It is not in time that you see or in time that you move or in time that you rest: yet you make what we see in time; you make time itself and the repose that comes when time ceases.

Ultimately, the *Confessions* is not about Augustine but about God. It is He alone who can lead us to the truth. That is why the book takes the form of a prayer: that is why it ends in the way it does:

> What man can teach another to understand this truth? What angel can teach it to an angel? What angel can teach it to a man? We must ask it of you, seek it in you; we must knock at your door. Only then shall we receive what we ask and find what we seek; only then will the door be opened to us.

Proba
Virgilian Cento (mid-4th century)

As we have seen already, some Christian authors thought very carefully about how they should respond to the inheritance of pagan literature they had received. In the fourth century, St Basil explained that when pagan writers "recount the words and deeds of good men, you should both love and imitate them, earnestly emulating such conduct. But when they portray base conduct, you must flee from them and stop up your ears, as Odysseus is said to have fled past the song of the sirens, for familiarity with evil writings paves the way for evil deeds. Therefore the soul must be guarded with great care, lest through our love for letters it receive some contamination unawares, as men drink in poison with honey." He then set out a wonderful image for his readers to hammer home his point:

> But on the other hand we shall receive gladly those passages in which they praise virtue or condemn vice. For just as bees know how to extract honey from flowers, which to men are agreeable only for their fragrance and color, even so here also those who look for something more than pleasure and enjoyment in such writers may derive profit for their souls. Now, then, altogether after the manner of bees must we use these writings, for the bees do not visit all the flowers without discrimination, nor indeed do they seek to carry away entire those upon which they light, but rather, having taken so much as is adapted to their needs, they let the rest go. So we, if wise, shall take from heathen books whatever befits us and is allied to the truth, and shall pass over the rest.

There were different ways of taking his advice to heart, but one of the most intriguing was demonstrated by Proba, who, as far as we know, was a fourth-century Roman noblewoman. Looking at the works of Virgil, the greatest of all Roman poets, she saw a foreshadowing of Christianity and so prayed to God that she might be able to "disclose the mysteries of the poet" and "declare that Virgil sang about the pious feats of Christ" (*Vergilium cecinisse loquar pia munera Christi*).

The way she did this was by extracting lines from the *Aeneid* to retell the story of salvation history, moving from the creation of the world (drawing on what Aeneas heard during his voyage to the Underworld) to the Fall (adapting the tragic story of Dido and Aeneas) to the death and resurrection of Christ. Her Virgilian cento is in effect a patchwork creation. Taking Virgil's poetry, she was able to supply a new dimension that had escaped even him.

Proba was not the first to write in this way and she certainly was not the last. The Empress Eudochia, who was a convert from paganism and wife of Theodosius II, composed a mammoth Christian cento from the works of Homer. Both of these poems have had a very mixed reception over the years, but they are now experiencing something of a critical comeback. More importantly, they can still speak to us about the glory of God, reminding us that what was old can again become new.

St Ephrem the Syrian
Hymns (mid-4th century)

There can be a tendency to regard the Church as essentially a Western institution, forgetting that it was born in Israel and then spread both eastwards and westwards. We have already considered Catholic books from around the world, including the work of St Isidore, who was born in Spain; St John Chrysostom, who hailed from what is now Turkey; and St Augustine, who reminds us of the importance of North Africa in the early Church. However, we have not yet ventured into Syria. With St Ephrem, one of the Doctors of the Church, we can now make good that gap.

It is significant that when Cassiodorus, who gave us our model of a liberal arts education, looked around for examples of good schools in the sixth century, he found them in Syria. Far from being cut off from the Catholic mainstream, it was, in fact, right at the heart of the Church: several popes from the sixth and early seventh centuries were born there, and this state of affairs changed only because of the rise and rapid expansion of Islam.

But Syria was an important center of the Faith even before the sixth century. As early as the early fourth century, St Ephrem helped spread the word of God through his writing, which brought theology and poetry together into a harmonious whole. As well as homilies in verse—now there's a challenge for every priest!—he also composed hundreds of hymns, of which over 400 have survived to this day, though few translations from his Syriac verses have found their way into English-language hymnbooks. One exception is "Strengthen for service, Lord, the hands":

Strengthen for service, Lord, the hands
that holy things have taken;
let ears that now have heard thy songs
to clamor never waken.

Lord, may the tongues which "Holy" sang
keep free from all deceiving;
the eyes which saw thy love be bright,
thy blessèd hope perceiving.

The feet that tread thy holy courts
from light do thou not banish;
the bodies by thy Body fed
with thy new life replenish.

St Ephrem was a great liturgical writer, blessed with a wonderful command of language that is perhaps more apparent in prose translations than in versifications. Take this striking set of images about Our Lady from a hymn "On the Nativity of Christ," for example: "The Lord entered her and became a servant; the Word entered her, and became silent within her; thunder entered her and his voice was still; the Shepherd of all entered her; he became a Lamb in her, and came forth bleating." Or these lines that take us from the first to the second Adam: "The trees of the Garden of Eden were given as food to the first Adam. For us, the gardener of the Garden in person made himself food for our souls."

St Ephrem was a wonderful writer who also witnessed with his life: as a deacon he served several bishops before his life was cut short by the plague in 373. Like Sor Juana Inéz de la Cruz, he caught the disease while tending the sick. As with so many of the authors featured in this book, he witnessed to God through everything he had: his life, his death, and his writing.

St Perpetua
The Martyrdom of Saints Perpetua and Felicitas (203)

Proba was not the only Christian woman writing in the early years of the Church. There is, for example, no more intriguing a piece of early Christian literature than the hugely popular *Martyrdom of Saints Perpetua and Felicitas*. It might seem to stretch credulity that St Perpetua wrote about her own martyrdom, but there are serious scholarly reasons for believing that the first-person accounts of Perpetua's imprisonment and visions were written by St Perpetua herself and that the rest of the book was completed by an eyewitness to her execution.

According to *The Martyrdom*, St Perpetua was still a catechumen when she was arrested and was baptized only in prison. She was about 22 years old and had recently married and given birth to a baby, whom she was able to nurse for at least some of her time behind bars.

The first-person sections of the book are a moving account of Perpetua's mental anguish. They describe, for example, the attempts of her pagan father to persuade her to make the necessary pagan sacrifices and her torment at being separated from her baby. But they are also an eloquent testimony to her resolution and joy. She told her father that, just as a vase cannot "be called by any other name than what it is," she "cannot be called anything except what I am, a Christian." She also found that her "prison became a palace" and that "she preferred to be there rather than anywhere else" when her baby was returned to her.

Perhaps the most remarkable passages, though, are the descriptions she gave of her visions. After praying to know whether she would suffer or be released, she was given a vision of a narrow ladder that only one person could climb at a time. Attached to this ladder was an array of weapons:

> There were swords, spears, hooks, daggers and spikes, so if anyone climbed up carelessly or without paying attention, he would be lacerated and his flesh stick to the iron weapons. And beneath the ladder itself lay a dragon of amazing size, which would reveal itself to those climbing up and try to frighten them into not climbing. But Saturus climbed up first. He later voluntarily handed himself in for our sake (because he had instructed us), although he had not been present when we were arrested. . . . And as if it were afraid of me, the dragon slowly put its head out from underneath that ladder. And as if it were the first step, I trod on its head and climbed up.

Climbing to the top of the ladder, she saw a tall shepherd, surrounded by thousands of white-clothed people, milking his sheep. Feeding her with the milk, he told her: "I am pleased you have come, my child."

This account was followed by other visions, including one of her brother in purgatory and later, after she released him with her prayers, in Paradise. St Perpetua also described the vision she received of her final battle in the arena. Knowing that she was about to be martyred, she was not downhearted: "I realized that I was going to fight against the devil, not wild animals, but I knew that I would be victorious."

She was indeed victorious, being executed by the sword with Felicitas, her slave, which is why we remember them in the Canon of the Mass to this day.

The Bible

To return to the Bible after reading many of the classics of Catholic literature from throughout the ages is to be struck once again by the amazing variety and power of the book (or, rather, books) from which so many writers drew their inspiration. St Isidore's *Etymologies* may have provided the people of his time with a library in one book, but his work was as nothing in comparison with the Sacred Scriptures. From poetry to biography, from history to vivid prophecy, the Bible really does have it all. Each of us will have our personal favorites—I love the Gospels, the humor of the Book of Jonah, the simple poignancy of the Book of Ruth, and the dazzling theology of St Paul's letters—but we can all return time and time again to this inexhaustible well, knowing that we will draw fresh nourishment each time. There can be no better way of finishing this survey of great literature than by returning to the Bible with fresh eyes, appreciating it as literature so that we can hear it as the inspired word of God.

When we return to the Bible we are reminded that, like the literature we have discovered already in this book, it too was written to point beyond itself. As Pope Benedict XVI reminded us in *Verbum Domini*, "The Christian faith is not a 'religion of the book'" in any simple sense. In the Church "we greatly venerate the sacred Scriptures," but, to quote St Bernard of Clairvaux, "Christianity is the 'religion of the word of God,' not of 'a written and mute word, but of the incarnate and living Word.'"

What does all this mean in practice? It means that we absolutely should read and re-read the Sacred Scriptures, but it also means that we should not make the mistake reflected most clearly by the Protestant churchman William

Chillingworth in the seventeenth century when he wrote: "The Bible, I say, the Bible only, is the religion of Protestants." The Bible is to be venerated, but it was always written to take us beyond the words to the Word himself.

That is why it is entirely right that we should finish our survey of great Catholic literature with the Bible, the greatest of all books. It shows us what Catholic literature can be, and it points us beyond mere books to the source of all goodness, beauty, and truth. As the Catechism tells us in paragraph 104, "In Sacred Scripture, the Church constantly finds her nourishment and her strength, for she welcomes it not as a human word, 'but as what it really is, the word of God.' 'In the sacred books, the Father who is in heaven comes lovingly to meet his children, and talks with them.'" What more could we possibly ask than that?

A Bibliographical Guide to Accessible Editions in English

1 Kyung-Sook Shin, *Please Look after Mom*. New York: Vintage, 2012
2 Cormac McCarthy, *The Road*. London: Picador, 2009
3 Les A. Murray, *New Collected Poems*. Manchester: Carcanet, 2003
4 George Mackay Brown, *Beside the Ocean of Time*. Edinburgh: Polygon, 2011
5 Muriel Spark, *The Prime of Miss Jean Brodie*. Harmondsworth: Penguin, 1975
6 Gabriela Mistral, Paul Burns, and Salvador Ortiz-Carboneres, *Gabriela Mistral: Selected Poems*. Oxford: Aris & Phillips, 2006
7 J.R.R. Tolkien, *The Lord of the Rings*. London: Unwin, 1978
8 Flannery O'Connor, *A Good Man is Hard to Find*. London: Faber, 2016
9 David Jones, *The Anathemata*. London: Faber, 2010
10 Evelyn Waugh, *Brideshead Revisited*. Harmondsworth: Penguin, 2016
11 Takashi Nagai, and William Johnston, *The Bells of Nagasaki*. Tokyo: Kodansha International, 2002
12 Ernest Hemingway, *A Farewell to Arms*. London: Arrow, 2004
13 Sigrid Undset, and Tina Nunnally, *Kristin Lavransdatter*. Harmondsworth: Penguin, 2005
14 Paul Claudel, Luigi Giussani, and Louise Morgan Sill, *The Tidings Brought to Mary*. Broomfield, CO: Human Adventure Books, 2009

15 G.K. Chesterton, *Charles Dickens*. Ware: Wordsworth Editions, 2007
16 Henryk Sienkiewicz, and C.J. Hogarth. *Quo Vadis?* London: J.M. Dent, 1952
17 Gerard Manley Hopkins, and Catherine Phillips, *Selected Poetry*. Oxford: OUP, 1998
18 John Henry Newman, *Callista, a Sketch of the Third Century*. London: Longmans, Green, and Co., 1890
19 Alessandro Manzoni, and Bruce Penman, *The Betrothed*. London: Penguin, 2016
20 François-René de Chateaubriand, and Walter J. Cobb, *Atala & René*. New York: Signet, 1962
21 Sor Juana Inés de la Cruz, René Domeier, and Patricia A. Peters, *The Divine Narcissus = El Divino Narciso*. Albuquerque, NM: University of New Mexico Press, 1998
22 Jonathan Chaves, *Singing of the Source: Nature and God in the Poetry of the Chinese Painter Wu Li*. Honolulu: University of Hawai'i Press, 1993
23 John Dryden, *Selected Poems*. London: Routledge, 2007
24 Hans Jakob Christoffel von Grimmelshausen, and J.A. Underwood, *Adventures of Simplicius Simplicissimus*. Harmondsworth: Penguin, 2018
25 Richard Crashaw, *Selected Poems: Secular and Sacred*. Manchester: Fyfield Books, 2013
26 Pedro Calderón de la Barca, and Bruce W. Wardropper, *The Prodigious Magician = El Mágico Prodigioso*. Potomac, MD: Studia Humanitatis, 1982
27 St Robert Southwell, Peter Davidson and Anne Sweeney, *Collected Poems*. Manchester: Fyfield Books, 2007
28 St John of the Cross, and Roy Campbell, *Poems of St John of the Cross*. London: Harvill Press, 1972
29 Stephen Knight, and Thomas H. Ohlgren, *Robin Hood and Other Outlaw Tales*. Kalamazoo, MI: Medieval Insti-

tute Publications, 1997; https://d.lib.rochester.edu/
teams/text/robin-hood-and-the-monk

30 Peter Happé, *English Mystery Plays*. Harmondsworth:
Penguin, 1975

31 A.C. Cawley, and J.J. Anderson, *Sir Gawain and the
Green Knight, Pearl, Cleanness, Patience*. London: Every-
man, 1991

32 Patrick J. Gallacher, *The Cloud of Unknowing*. Kalamazoo, MI: Medieval Institute Publications, 1997; https://
d.lib.rochester.edu/teams/publication/gallacher-the-
cloud-of-unknowing

33 Julian of Norwich, A.C. Spearing, and Elizabeth Spearing, *Revelations of Divine Love*. Harmondsworth: Penguin, 1998

34 A.C. Cawley, and J.J. Anderson, *Sir Gawain and the
Green Knight, Pearl, Cleanness, Patience*. London: Every-
man, 1991

35 Jacobus de Voragine, William Granger Ryan, and Eamon
Duffy, *The Golden Legend: Readings on the Saints*. Princeton, NJ: Princeton University Press, 2012

36 Dante Alighieri, and Henry Francis Cary, *The Divine
Comedy*. Ware: Wordsworth Editions, 2009

37 Robert Anderson, and Johann M. Moser, *The Aquinas
Prayer Book: The Prayers and Hymns of St Thomas
Aquinas*. Manchester, NH: Sophia Institute Press, 2000

38 Bernard Scudder, *Egil's Saga*. Harmondsworth: Penguin,
1997

39 Hildegard of Bingen, and Barbara Newman, *Symphonia:
a critical edition of the "Symphonia armonie celestium
revelationum" (Symphony of the Harmony of Celestial
Revelations)*. Ithaca: Cornell University Press, 1988

40 Chrétien de Troyes, Carleton Carroll, William W. Kibler,
Arthurian Romances. Harmondsworth: Penguin, 1991

41 Glyn Burgess, *The Song of Roland*. Harmondsworth: Penguin, 1990

42 Kevin Crossley-Holland, *The Anglo-Saxon World: An Anthology*. Oxford: OUP, 1990

43 Bede, Leo Shirley-Price, and R. E. Latham, *Ecclesiastical History of the English People*. Harmondsworth: Penguin, 1990

44 Isidore of Seville, Stephen A. Barney et al., *The Etymologies of Isidore of Seville*. Cambridge: Cambridge University Press, 2010

45 St John Chrysostom, Catharine P. Roth, and David Anderson, *On Marriage and Family Life*. Crestwood, NY: St. Vladimir's Seminary Press, 1997

46 St Augustine, and R. S. Pine-Coffin, *Confessions*. Harmondsworth: Penguin, 1961

47 I. M. Plant, *Women Writers of Ancient Greece and Rome*. London: Equinox Publishing, 2004

48 St Ephrem, and Kathleen E. McVey, *Ephrem the Syrian: Hymns*. Mahwah, NJ: Paulist Press, 1989

49 I. M. Plant, *Women Writers of Ancient Greece and Rome*. London: Equinox Publishing, 2004

50 The Revised Standard Version Catholic Edition of the Bible